Lucinda!
Enjoy!

MARTHA GROVER

The
End of
My Career

a Perfect Day book
© Martha Grover 2016
The moral right of the author has been asserted.

Portions of this book first appeared in very different form in *Somnambulist* *vols. 11, 24, 25, 26,* and *27.* "The Truth About Pheromones" was anthologized by Unknown Press in *In Case We Die.* The illustration of hard-boiled eggs first appeared on www.realpants.com.

The End of My Career / Martha Grover
ISBN: 978-0-9836327-5-7
Library of Congress Control Number: 2016950242

Second printing October 2016

Cover design by Aaron Robert Miller
Illustrations by Martha Grover
Photos courtesy Oregon DPSST
Perfect Day logo by Corinne Manning
Copyedited by Jessie Carver
Website by David Small

Printed by Worzalla in the United States of America
Set in Adobe Garamond and Hoefler Text at the IPRC

www.somnambulistzine.com
www.perfectdaypublishing.com

This book is dedicated to my parents and to the Sandy River.

Contents

Cleaning Jack's House

THE CIRCUMSTANCES UNDER WHICH I started cleaning Jack's house seemed a little like an intervention; a woman I met at a literary event emailed me in the late spring and asked if I was still taking on new housecleaning clients. Her friend Jack was a "total bachelor slob" and "he knew he needed help." I guess that's the first step ... knowing you need help. She wondered if she could give him my email.

Jack emailed me a few days later. We arranged a time for me to come over and clean his one-bedroom house in North Portland. "I'm sorry about the mess," he wrote. I told him not to worry about it; all of my clients, even the very tidy ones, were constantly apologizing for their mess, however small. Clean people hire housecleaners, not slobs. Slobs don't care.

A week later I dragged my supplies up to the front door and fished for the hidden house key under the mat. Even though both Jack and his friend had warned me about the state of his house, I still wasn't prepared for what I saw. Piles of empty Amazon boxes covered the ground. Every surface in the living room and dining room was covered in papers, empty boxes, bowls of dog food and water, packing material, bike parts, tubs of protein mix, stacks of receipts, mud-caked race numbers, safety pins, three bikes, dog hair, ant traps, half-empty grocery bags, dirty dishes, and books. I stood in the doorway and took it all in. A truly messy house is a thing of wonder—you so rarely see it. Messy people don't host dinner parties.

I took a deep breath, made sure all of my supplies were inside the front door, and got to work.

I spent the first hour just breaking down cardboard boxes. Several of the boxes from Amazon seemed to have been punched in with a fist. The contents had been grabbed almost magically out, leaving the receipt and the packing inside with hardly any opening. I wondered about the kind of person who couldn't even be bothered to open a box properly. I stacked them in the living room, in a pile nearly as tall as myself.

The next forty minutes were spent returning objects to their proper places. I discovered that Jack often didn't empty out his paper grocery bags when he got home—several otherwise empty bags contained a single forgotten apple, or a can of beans, or a power bar. Books were scattered around the house. I found them everywhere, under piles of newspapers and boxes, under his sheets, and in the bathroom. He was a fan of science fiction and self-help. I returned the paperbacks one by one to the built-in bookcases on either side of the fireplace. I had to stop myself from organizing them into sections. I didn't have time and that wasn't my job.

In his bedroom, I stacked his piles of clothes as neatly as I could, although it was impossible to tell the clean from the dirty without smelling them, which was something I refused to do; you have to draw the line somewhere.

As I cleaned, I appraised the mess. Jack was a slob for sure, but he wasn't a hoarder. I knew what a hoarder's house looked like; I'd spent the last six months of my previous relationship binge-watching that reality show alone in my office while I made collages out of old magazines and slowly drained my bank account. No, there was nothing pathological about the mess. You could tell that he meant to throw the trash out and go through the mail, he just hadn't gotten around to it. Jack was preoccupied. With what, I didn't know.

With sweat streaming down my face, starving, and my back extremely sore, I barely made it out of Jack's house in the four-hour timeframe I'd promised him. I thought I did a pretty damn good job, though, considering the state of the house when I'd arrived. I called him from my car, shoving a piece of jerky into my mouth. Through bites I left him a voice message. "Hello Jack, this is Martha. You can PayPal me. Next time there are other areas of the house that I'll be able to clean, but I didn't get to them this time. Let me know if you ever want me to take your shower curtain down and bleach it, in like the backyard or something."

Later that evening I got an email from Jack, who told me I was a miracle worker. I smiled. It felt good to know I had made his day better.

I came back in two weeks and the house looked almost as bad as it did the first time. I was annoyed that Jack hadn't even moved the stack of cardboard boxes from the living room into his recycling bin. I spent another four hurried hours cleaning. This time I left the boxes on the front porch, hoping that the visible mess would prompt him to put them in his bin. I could have done it myself but, like I said, I had to draw the line somewhere and its location was often arbitrary.

It went on like this for several months over the summer. The house was always only incrementally cleaner than the last time I'd been there. Jack never asked me to clean his moldy, soap-spattered shower curtain, a task I'd decided was above my pay grade unless specifically asked. He didn't stop throwing his clothes on the floor. One time I showed up and he hadn't even bothered to flush his toilet. It was filled with a huge pile of shit. "Oh my god," I said to no one. I couldn't believe he'd just left it like that, knowing that I was coming over to clean that morning. I flushed the toilet, but of course it was all plugged up. There was no plunger in the bathroom and I thought for a minute about just leaving it that way. This wasn't in my self-defined job description. But, I decided, leaving it there would be just as bad as what he'd done to me. I could imagine him coming home to a spotless home and then discovering the toilet filled to the brim with his own half-dissolved shit. I knew now that I had to plunge it because if I didn't, it would seem like I was leaving it there on purpose, like a slap in his face, which of course would be an accurate assessment. This could be the crucible by which our whole working relationship was tested. Did I want the job or not?

I looked all over the house and finally found a plunger in the basement. I walked to the toilet, stood over it, and thought to myself: *This is what you are paid to do, Martha.* But I knew that Jack probably wouldn't even remember that he'd left the toilet this way. That's the thing about dirty clients—they don't notice when you do a good job or a bad job, because they are people with different standards, the kind of people who don't even realize their housecleaner is going to see the giant crap they've left in the toilet. I thought, *If I leave it there he'll probably think it was my poop.* So really, I was screwed either way.

Nothing so bad as that ever happened again, and I continued to work for and wonder about Jack, someone I would never meet but grew to know so much about. He seemed to have purchased every book ever written on the subject of depression. Whether he ever read them, I don't know. He was also taking various antidepressants, which he left lying around in the kitchen. I put them away in the cupboard next to his countless bottles of vitamins. He was a compulsive cycler; he owned at least four bicycles and raced them competitively. He was also obsessed with health. I never saw any alcohol, potato chips, or any other junk food in his house. Except that I would often find empty plastic pints of a certain kind of gourmet ice cream in the kitchen sink, sometimes as many as ten, scraped clean of their contents.

Jack ate in bed, with his dog. The sheets were often filthy with food and hair. Next to the bed was a pile of candles and animal bones, a big bunch of burned sage. Candle wax was melted all over the house.

I imagined Jack to be chronically depressed, a resigned bachelor, definitely either celibate or unashamed of the state of his house. My main function seemed to be keeping him from drowning in a sea of empty cardboard boxes and ice cream containers. At the same time, unlike most of my other clients, Jack didn't try to put on a show for me. He didn't "pre-clean." And in this way he was the most vulnerable of them all.

Then one day there were tomato and basil plants on the front porch. *Huh,* I thought. *That's new.* I opened the front door and the house was neat. The stacks of screws, bolts, pens and paper clips and receipts on every surface had been sorted and sifted. The recycling had been taken out. I walked into his bedroom and the anteroom, behind the curtain, where I had hidden his bikes and dirty laundry, had been completely cleaned out and mopped. Off to the left, a work area had been set up with a computer and printer. Jack's cycling awards were resting on the windowsill. A picture of him with a middle school track team was resting in a broken frame on the desk. It was the only picture I'd seen of Jack. I bent over and looked at it. He was a tall attractive man, although his expression in the photo looked tired. He was a track coach. *Good for him*, I thought.

That September, Jack left a note mentioning that he wanted me to come once a month to clean instead of every other week because he had a friend staying with him. *This friend must be someone he wants to impress*, I thought. I shrugged and headed into the living room to put on my apron and grab my feather duster. Near the couch I saw a rolled up blanket, a pillow, and a small green backpack.

Luckily, there was still work to do. As I made my way around the living room dusting and cleaning, I found a note written in neat, rigid handwriting on a yellow legal pad. It was a list. I stopped and looked at it. I felt guilty snooping, but I couldn't help it. It was just sitting there on the now very tidy buffet as if on display. At the top it said: *CONTRACT FOR JASON / HOUSE RULES. 1. Jason to remain clean and sober while staying with Jack. 2. Jason to do twenty hours of work a week on the house* ... and the list continued with fifteen or so rules, each written in what seemed to me very deliberate, formal language.

The bottom of the list was an explanation of consequences if Jason did not follow the rules—mainly that he would be kicked out. And then at the bottom of the page, both Jack and Jason had signed, printed, and dated the contract.

I felt stupid that I'd missed it before. Jack was a recovering addict. The depression, the compulsive exercise, even the empty pints of ice cream in the sink all fit together in a constellation of habits and coping mechanisms; I figured he'd been sober for a couple of years. And now he was giving back by hosting a fellow addict. Who knows—it was all speculation anyway. I'd been cleaning Jack's house for about six months, but what did I really know about the man?

Mainly I was worried that Jason, the down-on-his-luck houseguest, was going to work me out of a job. This time it only took me three hours to clean Jack's house. That was a twenty-five dollar pay cut. Damn you, Jason. Thanks for nothing.

It didn't last for long, though. A few months later, in mid-winter, Jason was gone and the house was noticeably messier. I breathed a sigh of relief; my job was secure. On the other hand I felt sorry for Jack. Would he slip into his bad habits, would I start finding cereal bowls and his open laptop under the bed sheets?

Then, several weeks after Jason left, Jack emailed me. He wanted me to dust the ceiling fan above his bed. I thought this was odd, given he'd never made a specific request before. As far as I knew he didn't notice half of the special things I did for him. Why start now with the special requests? Especially when his shower curtain was still orange with mold and crusty white with soap scum? I climbed on his bed and cleaned his ceiling fan, sending cascades of dust onto his bedspread, sneezing.

One day in March, I started my usual routine, dusting the living room and neatening the table in the dining room. I walked into the bathroom, where a Post-it was stuck to the mirror: "Hi Sexy."

My eyes focused on myself then, in the mirror, red-faced and a little sweaty, in my sports bra and blue cotton shirt with the bleach stains around the collar. Obviously the note wasn't directed at me. I looked around. There was another note stuck to the inside of the shower curtain. "I can't wait to come back tonight and fuck you silly."

Jack had a girlfriend.

Suddenly the ceiling fan request made sense. His girl-friend probably mentioned how dusty it was—he couldn't have come up with that on his own. I smiled. And as I continued cleaning, I was surprised at how happy I was for Jack. He was having good sex. He had a lady around that left him cheesy notes on his bathroom mirror. I couldn't stop grinning. Good for him; he deserved it.

I started finding sex toys around the house. A tiny whip by the bed. An erotic book in the living room. And the house was generally cleaner every month. The clutter was under control and there were fewer empty ice cream pints in the sink. The last two months I cleaned for him, I didn't find a single cardboard box on the floor. Jack started emailing me, telling me he didn't need me that month. Once he even forgot to leave the key for me and I had to turn around and go home. But this wasn't any of that "a woman makes a house a home" bullshit. Any woman who would leave a sexy note on a shower curtain that filthy wasn't doing any housekeeping for him. I knew it was only a matter of time before he laid me off, and I was okay with that.

The Truth
About Pheromones

WE MET AT A CHINESE RESTAURANT on Hawthorne. He introduced himself and then he told me I looked nice. This was my fifth date with someone I'd met on OkCupid, and this was the first time that any of my dates had complimented me about anything. It felt nice. I was surprised, actually, by how nice it felt.

On our second date we got drunk at a bar. He told me, "You're so smart it's kind of intimidating." Apparently the evidence for this was that I've watched a lot of nature documentaries and had decided to share with him fun facts about fratricide and pseudo-penises among female spotted hyenas in Africa. I changed the subject after he said this. It made me a little suspicious; men who are intimidated by a woman's intelligence scare me. There is a difference between being scared and being intimidated. Besides, I didn't believe his statement.

We made out in his car and then in my car. It felt good to kiss someone. I knew I would have hickies and bruises on my breasts later but it seemed worth it at the time.

He asked me if I wanted to come home with him. "I can't," I said. "I don't have my medication with me."

"What medicine?" he said.

"If I don't take it, it'll ruin my day tomorrow," I said.

"Well come over on Sunday," he said. "And bring your medicine."

I didn't tell him that not taking my medication would actually ruin two days total. And that if I didn't take it for three days my body would start to shut down. And that there is a big difference between medicine and medication.

"Okay, we'll hang out on Sunday," I said.

That Sunday, as I merged onto I-84, I turned on the radio to a program about cranes. They were interviewing a biologist who'd worked his whole life trying to protect endangered cranes. He explained how one of the biggest crane populations lives in the DMZ between North and South Korea, and how they have been an important part of Japanese and other cultural traditions.

The interviewer asked the biologist why cranes were so loved by us humans. Cranes look like humans, he replied. They have long legs like us, they live as long as us (at least in captivity), they dance like us. In fact, he said, cranes are one of the few animals that truly dance like humans.

I wondered what the cranes are thinking when they do their complicated mating dance. Are they worried they won't remember the steps? Or are they in lockstep like soldiers doing drills? One time on the radio, I heard a woman from the Freedom Singers say that if it were not for music, the civil rights movement might never have happened. The music, the ritual, the lyrics and the rhythm of it, the rigid form of the songs, gave the protestors courage.

We had sushi. I finished a bottle of wine at his apartment. He sat down on the couch next to me and started kissing my face, my neck. He took off my shirt and started kissing my breasts. We went down the hallway into his dark bedroom. He asked me if I wanted the lights on or off, which seemed irrelevant to me. I told him to keep them off.

He wanted me to be on top, not surprising, considering he was overweight and from what I gathered, led a rather sedentary life. The truth is that I've never been very good at being on top, especially when I don't know someone very well. I start to feel self-conscious. I got on top anyway. But after a bit, it just didn't feel right. It wasn't fun. I rolled off him.

"What's wrong?" he said.

I sighed. "I don't know, this is the first sex I've had in a year," I said. "I guess I'm just trying to wrap my head around it. That's all." This was partly true. What was I doing here anyway? All of a sudden the scenario seemed wrong. Not what I'd pictured.

He didn't say anything. Both of us just lay there for a few minutes.

"I'm sorry," I said.

"That's okay." A few more minutes of silence. Finally he got up and walked out of the room. I heard the toilet flush and he came back and got in bed. *I do want to have sex though*, I said to myself.

"Here," I said. "Get on top of me."

"What?"

"Just lay on top of me."

"Are you sure?"

I nodded. He got on top of me but I could tell he was still tense, propping himself up slightly on his elbows.

"No, you need to relax," I said.

"I'm going to crush you."

"No, you're not. Don't worry, just relax." I breathed in

and out fully, to show him that he wasn't going to crush me, as men often think they are going to do. I wanted to show him that I was going to be fine.

I've always felt this position to be very relaxing. That is, lying under a large man. It reminds me of Temple Grandin's book *Animals in Translation,* where she talks about how being autistic, for her, is like being a cow. When she was a teenager she built herself a compression box that would press down on her sides when she climbed inside it. If she was feeling anxious, it calmed her down. This is the same effect being in tightly packed herds has on cows. Farmers put cows in compression devices before they give them their immunization shots so they won't get too anxious.

After a few seconds, I felt his body relaxing on top of me.

"Here, get inside of me," I said. And we had sex.

He came, but I didn't. I asked him to finish me off with his hands. He put his hand on my clitoris. He started rubbing, and then paused. "Do you like up and down or round and round?" he asked.

This question annoyed me, like he was asking me how I wanted my steak cooked. "I don't care," I said.

After I came, we talked a little bit in his too-soft bed. I told him I couldn't have children. "The only reason I even have a period," I said, "is because I take birth control. I take it just for the estrogen. And even then I still don't have a period sometimes."

"You're like a unicorn," he said.

"What do you mean?"

"A woman who doesn't have her period, a unicorn."

I still didn't really understand what he meant by this, although I could tell that it was insensitive. We lay there in silence.

"You don't want to have kids," I said eventually.

"No. There's enough people on this planet." He sighed and looked up at the ceiling.

"Yeah, it's insane," I said, becoming a little animated. "It's terrifying to think about, actually, how many people are living. I recently visited a website that calculates all the births and deaths on Earth every ten seconds. It was horrifying." I rolled over so I was facing him and put one arm over his body.

"Yeah, what we need is another black plague," he whispered into my face.

"That's really sexy," I said.

We both started giggling. Our bellies touched, and I could feel his stomach jump up and down. We both laughed for what seemed like a long time.

I asked him if he wanted to go to the Sandy River with me the next day. He said yes. *This plan is going to work perfectly*, I thought. I had dinner plans that night in Portland anyway. I could go to the river and then drop him off at his apartment on the way back into town. Theoretically I was supposed to be working from home, but I could always do that work later. I had my whole day planned out. I said goodnight.

He fell asleep fast and started snoring, loudly. Eventually, I moved into the living room and tried to sleep on his couch. But I could hear his snoring even from the couch and so only intermittently slept through the night.

In the morning we went to breakfast. The conversation lagged. I asked him if there was anything he wanted to know about me. He asked me what I thought about the new batch of superhero movies that had recently been produced. I didn't quite believe he'd actually just asked me this and so we talked about the new batch of superhero movies until I said that they usually make these kinds of movies for a global audience and that they had to give the back stories of the superheroes so people in China would understand what was going on. Then he looked as if I had just told him that Santa Claus wasn't real, maybe because he thought I was wrong, maybe because as a white male he couldn't imagine a world in which he wasn't the target audience, and so I changed the subject.

The sky was still overcast when we left the breakfast place. "Maybe we shouldn't go to the river," I said, looking doubtfully at the sky.

"Yeah, besides we both stayed up late. Maybe it would be better to just relax today."

I nodded, even though going to the river did seem like relaxing to me. The only problem was that now that I wasn't going to the river, I didn't want to go home to Gresham and work from home, only to have to drive back into Portland that night. I also didn't want to go to a coffee shop because I find them uncomfortable to hang out in for more than an hour. "Well, then do you mind if I hang out at your house today and get some work done?" I asked.

He said that would be fine. But when we got back to his house, I was so tired from lack of sleep that I fell asleep on his couch while he went out to run some errands. My phone rang in the middle of the nap. I stumbled into his bedroom where my phone was charging on the floor. It was my publisher, Michael. "Did I wake you up?"

"Uh ...."

"It sounds like I woke you up."

I admitted that he had woken me up. Michael asked what I'd been up to. I wanted to tell him that I'd had sex for the first time in a year the night before with a man that I wasn't even attracted to. But I didn't say this because I was sitting on the man's bed at the time and it just seemed wrong, and mean. And then I felt trapped in his apartment. Hearing Michael's voice snapped me out of a trance, made me question the whole scenario. What was I doing here anyway?

"I'll tell you about it later," I said.

I could have gathered my things and left, but instead, I got off the phone and went back to sleep on the couch.

My date woke me up later and we had a Caesar salad together and watched a nature documentary about humpback whales. We had sex again, this time on the couch.

After we got dressed, I sat back down on the couch and started doing computer work for my boss at the coffee table.

He got on his computer and started looking at photoshopped pictures of cats on Reddit, periodically tugging at his penis through his pajama pants. And this was when I started to feel weird about seeing him again in the future, not just the fact that I was here now, in his apartment, instead of at home or at a coffee shop. It was becoming clear to me that this guy wasn't anyone I really ever wanted to see again. There were several things that weren't right to me and I started to tick them off in my head. First of all, his question about the superhero movies when he could have asked me something about me. The fact that he hadn't done any artwork since he graduated from design school two years ago and seemed uninterested in creating anything ever again. The fact that he seemed uninterested when I showed him my artwork. The fact that he was unmotivated to lose weight.

Plus, his apartment smelled like he'd spilled an entire bottle of cologne onto the dirty carpet. The bathroom smelled like cigarettes and when I asked him why, he said that it was his neighbors, and had something to do with the pipes. I felt like he was lying. He told me that he didn't think hairy underarms on women were sexy. He kept using words incorrectly, like "conductive" instead of "conducive."

Nevertheless, I had sex with him one more time before I left.

Afterwards, after I had gotten home and taken a shower, after I'd emailed him and told him that I wasn't going to be hanging out with him again, I couldn't figure out why I had had sex with him to begin with. Perhaps the first time made sense. But then, why didn't I just leave? Was having sex two more times with a guy I wasn't that into better than a commute to Gresham and back? Better than sitting in a coffee shop all day instead of his stinky apartment? I didn't have a good answer. And to not have an answer wasn't acceptable. I was an adult after all, I should have an answer as to why I do, or don't, have sex with someone.

In medicine, when they can't come up with a cause for a disease, they call it idiopathic. I've always thought the word sounded like idiot. The idiot's path. I'd had idiopathic sex. Had I been infected with a mind-control parasite, like the ones that make ants walk up stalks of grass so they can get eaten by prey and then pooped out to begin the parasite's life cycle all over again?

All through the next week, I thought about it and thought about it. Somehow I'd become locked into this mating dance with this guy and it had become impossible to extricate myself. Maybe we were like those cranes. Or like those African beetles that one of my sisters had told me about. The huge males mate with the smaller females, who then burrow into the ground to lay their eggs. The male beetle stays up at the top, guarding the entrance from other males. But there are also some males of the same species who are quite small, much smaller than the other males. These small males don't bother battling it out for access to the entrance to the female's lair. Instead they dig an alternate passage down to where the female is waiting, mate with her, and get out unscathed. I liked the idea that members of the same species can have radically different mating strategies, but I didn't like where it put me as the female: passive, just waiting for a beetle to come and impregnate me.

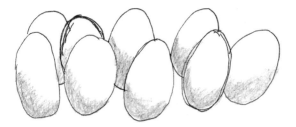

Maybe my idiopathic sex had something to do with hormones. Five years ago I found out I had idiopathic Cushing's Disease, and for a bunch of reasons that I don't have the energy to explain, I'm now taking every hormone a person can take except for testosterone. My endocrinologist told me that I'd probably had low estrogen since puberty. I'd only started taking estrogen pills a little before I'd broken up with my ex-boyfriend. Maybe it was the estrogen that made me have sex with this guy.

I thought about it, how it used to take me forever to orgasm and how when I did, it was okay. Now that I take estrogen, my orgasms are much, much better. I told my sister Sarah about this. "I think it's the estrogen," I'd said.

"Well you're in your thirties," she said. "You're at your sexual peak." Sarah is a nurse and is regarded in our family as being a medical authority.

"Yeah, but does that account for the quality of orgasm?" I asked her.

She said yes. I doubted her. Something about this explanation didn't seem right. But if it was right, did this also mean that I was due for lots more sex with men I wasn't really attracted to? The thought horrified me.

I drove into Portland for a teacher training, and ran into a friend in the parking lot. She chatted with me outside while I smoked a cigarette. I told her about my experience with the guy from OkCupid. "Ugh, I don't know why I had sex with that guy," I muttered.

"Well, why did you?"

"I guess I felt kind of pressured into it," I said, and the moment I said it I knew it wasn't true. In no way was I pressured into it. But it was easier to say this than to say that I didn't know.

I went home and did some research about the rise in women's libido in their thirties. First of all, the rise of libido in women in their thirties is entirely self-reported. Furthermore, all libido really means is sex drive, not the actual pleasure derived from sex. The studies also imply sex with another person. Not masturbation. There are so many factors, like confidence, self-esteem, and emotional maturity that play a part here, that I wasn't convinced that my estrogen level had anything to do with libido. My libido has remained constant over the last fifteen years or so. Besides, most women have constant estrogen levels until menopause. As usual, I couldn't compare myself with normal women, at least not hormonally.

I thought back on the last ten years of my sex life. Before I was diagnosed with Cushing's, in my early and mid twenties, sex, to me, had been either an entirely emotional affair, or else athletic—akin to asking someone to play a rigorous game of badminton with me. I never felt that some invisible tractor beam was pulling me towards someone. I'd always been in control. It was always a decision I had made, a line in the sand. However, this recent sex had been something different; I didn't feel in control at all. It had just happened. I somehow had lost all my personal agency and I wasn't sure why. Could the estrogen have made me act this way?

And then I remembered pheromones, those invisible chemicals known to mysteriously influence human sexuality. They've always seemed like mumbo jumbo to me. It's not as if I don't believe in science. Science saves my life every day in the form of little white pills synthesized from porcine hormones. It's just that the existence of pheromones has never jived with my own lived experience. In all my sexual encounters, I have never felt the invisible pull of someone's body. Everything has always been very visible.

A week later, at a family baby shower, I talked with my cousin Donald and told him I didn't know why I had had sex with this guy.

"I don't really believe in pheromones," I said. "But I have no other way to explain it."

"Oh, I totally believe in pheromones," he said. "Haven't you ever been around someone that you're attracted to and you don't know why?"

I considered it. *No*, I thought. *I know why I'm attracted to someone. It's always something. It doesn't have to be rational. But I always know why.*

"You know how I knew Sarah was into me?" he said, gesturing towards his wife at the other end of the couch. "We met each other at a funeral. This was when I was working out a ton. I was totally ripped. She wouldn't stop touching me. I gave her my phone number and said, 'Call me.' She was talking about how busy she was all the time. I just handed her my number and said, 'Call me when you're not busy.'"

This anecdote didn't prove anything. Touching was a kind of visual cue, after all. Pheromones were an olfactory cue.

I must not have looked convinced, because Donald went on. He described a study where the scientists had men work out on treadmills until they were dripping with sweat. They took the men's sweaty shirts and put them in sealed jars. Then they had a young woman smell the shirts and rate them on a scale from one to ten on "attractiveness." The shirt that she rated lowest, that had made her gag upon smelling it, turned out to be her father's shirt. This was supposed to prove that pheromones signal to offspring that certain males are off limits, sexually speaking. If it was true, it could mean that much of our behavior is not necessarily pre-ordained but out of our conscious control.

I thought the subject needed further investigation. Maybe I didn't even know what pheromones were.

Later that night, after the conversation with Donald, when the rest of my family sat down to watch TV, I went to my bedroom and got online and started researching pheromones—because if the cause wasn't estrogen, maybe it was pheromones?

FACTS ABOUT PHEROMONES:

1. Pigs are used to sniff out truffles because truffles emit an odor very similar to pig sex pheromones.

2. Estrogen, although not a pheromone, is the oldest hormone on the planet.

3. Although testosterone is often given to postmenopausal women to increase sex drive, our bodies can synthesize testosterone from estrogen and so the efficacy of this treatment is in question.

4. Humans as a species are much more susceptible to visual cues as opposed to olfactory cues. I wonder what dating is like for blind people. I once dated a man with no sense of smell. As far as I can tell this had no effect on our sex life.

5. Women's periods probably don't sync for pheromonal reasons, if at all. This theory, that women who live together sync their menstrual periods, is known as the McClintock effect and the study that coined this term has been impossible to reproduce. This effect is probably just a result of the variability of women's periods in general, because if they live together their periods will inevitably overlap to some degree. I can back this up with personal experience. I have six sisters and our periods were never synced for any real length of time. Thank god.

6. The results from many pheromone studies, like the one Donald told me about, cannot be reproduced. Or if they are reproduced the results are of no statistical significance.

7. As it turns out, there isn't much scientific evidence for pheromones in humans after all. Their existence and the role they play in mating in humans are contested within scientific communities. Every article I read seemed to doubt their existence as a factor in sexual attraction and behavior. I was

surprised that they had somehow found their way so completely into our everyday conversations. Maybe it was because people had been mistaking pheromones for hormones. Hormones affect an individual's own behavior, not the behavior of others. Pheromones are chemicals secreted by the body that affect the behavior of others. Somehow it's easier to blame pheromones than it is to blame hormones, I guess. Easier to blame someone else than to blame ourselves.

I emerged from my bedroom and went out to the living room on my parents' side of the house, where my brother, my sister-in-law, my parents, and my sister-in-law's mother were all watching the Miss America Pageant on TV.

I told them it pained me to see so many fake blondes on screen. "I'm a natural blonde," I said, "and all these women have such obviously fake blond hair … it's just kind of annoying."

"Well, they're doing something right," my dad said.

"What do you mean?"

"It's a strategy that seems to work."

I wondered if watching the Miss America Pageant was the best thing for me to be doing at that moment. Watching one Barbie doll after another parade across the screen in their bathing suits was just depressing me further.

We had the sound off on the TV. As the contestants came out in formal wear, we started critiquing each gown. Raeann, my brother's mother-in-law, is a biologist, and so I started sharing with her some of my recent discoveries regarding pheromones.

"It's been proven that symmetrical faces are more attractive," she said, pointing at the screen, her face perking up at the mention of science.

"I just read something about that today," I told her. "The reason, supposedly, that we are attracted to symmetrical faces is that it's supposed to demonstrate how an organism can maintain symmetry while developing under stressors."

My sister-in-law scrunched up her face. "Well, I don't think that's true for me. I am usually attracted to people with unusual faces. Or what about those Japanese flower arrangements that are lopsided?"

"There have also been studies that show that animals are attracted to novelty, because these traits strengthen the gene pool," I replied confidently. "You have to let new physical traits into the gene pool, otherwise things get too inbred."

Even in saying it, I knew my reply was too pat an answer. In this line of thinking everything had a biological reason. It implied that we're all just genetically preprogrammed robots. But that can't be true. Or at least I didn't want it to be true, even if it absolved me of any personal responsibility.

I thought back to that first date at the Chinese restaurant. How he'd told me that I looked nice. I realized that there *had* been a line in the sand after all. I had made the decision to have sex with him. I'd made the decision right then and there. It was the compliment. The compliment was the secret ingredient, the magic words, the strange, unseen force.

I sat down on the couch, a blur of slender bodies moving across my line of vision. I remembered another couch. A year, almost to the day, before this date I'd sat on my boyfriend's couch weeping, while he told me the reason we weren't having sex was because he wasn't attracted to me anymore.

Through gritted teeth, I'd told him that we should break up. I was too proud to say anything else.

I'd spent the next year slowly reassembling my self-esteem. A whole year marked by bouts of depression and joy, a whole year, before walking into that Chinese restaurant, indulging in long navel-gazing sessions of regret and bitterness. So, sitting there at the table in my black dress and push-up bra, I must have looked like low-hanging fruit.

What I mean to say is that I must have looked desperate. Because what I'd really done is spent a whole year trying to deny that I'd let one person so completely destroy my self-confidence, that I'd let another person have that much control over me. Instead of facing this, I'd pretended to be fine.

Pheromones don't exist. There's no mysterious biological factor controlling our actions and desires. Other people do have control over me, but in a way I hadn't let myself believe. All this talk of pheromones, hormones, and animal behavior was just a smoke screen.

What had really happened was this: I'd done something that I wasn't proud of, that I regretted. I wasn't ready to be vulnerable with another person, and so I had chosen to have sex with someone I didn't care about and then write about it as a way of making myself feel better. Even sadder is that I wasn't self-aware enough to even cop to it, so I had tried to blame it on my birth control pills or pheromones.

Someone I loved didn't want to have sex with me anymore and so I had sex with someone who wanted to have sex with me, but who didn't love me and who I didn't love.

We turned off the pageant before they announced the winner. The next morning I heard that the Indian-American Miss New York was the new Miss America. All those fake blondes, their strategy hadn't paid off after all. And this made me happy.

The Undercover Cruise

My sister Sarah gave us a few hints before we boarded. "There'll be a lot of old people on the boat," she said. "And don't tell anyone what you paid—it bothers people to know you only paid five hundred dollars for the trip."

The truth was, my father and I hadn't paid anything for the cruise; Sarah had actually paid for us to go, a detail that was lost on my self-centered twenty-one-year-old brain. She told us that we could pay her back later, something I never did, and still feel guilty about to this day.

My father and I were bound for British Columbia. It was a last-minute thing; Sarah, who was a bartender on the cruise ship, had gotten us a "friends and family" deal. The company she worked for was a small ecotourism line, each ship holding only sixty or so passengers. They specialized in whale watching and nature hikes, taking trips to British Columbia, Alaska, the Galapagos, Baja California, and Antarctica.

He and I were the only ones in the family with the flexibility to go; he was able to get the time off his work as an electrician, and I had just quit my job waiting tables at a diner back home and was about to move to Eugene to start school at the University of Oregon. Even though the trip was up Canada's western shore, in 2001 we didn't need passports to cross the border, which was convenient because we didn't have any.

We boarded the ship in Seattle and were shown to our small cabin with two twin beds and a toilet in the shower. Sarah hugged us in the hallway outside our door, overjoyed to have us there and to introduce us to all the coworkers she'd spent the last year with and had been writing home about.

For my part, I had no idea what we were getting ourselves into. We'd done no research into the cruise company. All we knew was that Sarah was enjoying the job and it had helped get her out of the rut she'd been in, working at the diner.

We didn't really know who or what the fellow passengers would be. And to be truthful, I hadn't a clue what I was myself at the time. I'd no real perspective of wealth, having grown up sheltered, in a small Oregon town, not realizing that my childhood had been spent at the desperate edges of the lower middle class, on and off food stamps and unemployment. My parents were raising seven children, my father was intermittently employed for much of my childhood, and neither of them had a college degree. At twenty-one all I knew was that I resented "rich people," who, in hindsight, were merely middle class, a distinction defined by me as having such things as: a nice house, a family trip to Disneyland, orthodontia, or the funding of college education. I had had my teeth fixed and was going to college, but these were luxuries that my grandmother and uncle had paid for, just like this trip was being paid for by Sarah.

27

We were escorted to the lounge where Sarah made us drinks. We sat down at a table with two older couples. One couple was from Brazil, the other from somewhere on the East Coast.

"Wow. Brazil! That's amazing!" said my father. This is common phrasing for my father, who is both curious and easily impressed.

"Have you been to Brazil?" the man asked.

"I've never been out of the country!" my father exclaimed.

I was a little embarrassed by this. But if it was amusing or interesting to the other couples, their faces didn't betray any emotion. They changed the subject rather abruptly to the kind of weather we'd be having that week and asked us no further questions about ourselves.

We chatted for a bit until the lounge was full, everyone had a drink, and the captain appeared and made a speech. The sun was setting as we left Seattle and made our way north into the darkness.

When I walked into the dining room the next morning, I saw that all the meals were going to be served at communal tables. I realized that this trip would require a marathon of small talk. There wasn't any alternative, no quiet space to eat in peace. And it wasn't just this first meal that frightened me, it was the anticipation of twenty-one more shared meals. This scenario would prove simple for my father, a natural extrovert, but I was preemptively exhausted. That morning my father and I sat down at the first table where we could find seats together.

The talk over breakfast centered around other vacations and cruises the couples had taken. One couple was talking about their trip to Turkey a few years earlier. "We bought all these amazing rugs," said the woman. "But when we brought them back to our cabin on Lake Michigan they didn't match any of the furniture so we *had* to get rid of it all and buy new furniture for the whole place!" This elicited laughs all around. I was confused. Apparently it had been a joke.

"You've been to Turkey?" I said. "That must have been interesting!"

The man turned to me and said under his breath, "Yes, if you ever go and buy rugs in Turkey, you must be careful. Otherwise those guys will cheat you." It seemed a bizarre statement to make. I couldn't imagine ever being in the position to haggle over rug prices in Turkey. I was both uncomfortable and entertained. I nodded.

As we made our way up the coast, we got to know our fellow passengers better. Many were from the East Coast. All of them were retired. The couple from Brazil were retired pharmaceutical executives. There was a retired corporate lawyer who had brought his three adult children with him. These three were all in their late thirties, unmarried and without children. My father remarked on this, asked if the matriarch was worried about her children's infertility. They seemed unconcerned. The son had been already a little too familiar with me. He was handsome, but it struck me as creepy the way he stared and lavished compliments on me.

"So, how are you two related?" the corporate lawyer's wife asked us at lunch.

"This is my daughter," said my dad.

"Oh! Your daughter!" she laughed. "All of us were speculating on your relationship." She looked at me. "We thought since you two were sharing a cabin you might be a child bride." Again, everyone laughed. I was mortified.

We landed on Vancouver Island and went on a hike in

the forest. It reminded me of the forests in Oregon: cedar and ferns. The guide pointed out all the plants I had grown up with and knew the names of already. One of the ladies asked me what I wanted to do with my English degree after I graduated. "I think I'll be a teacher," I said.

"Good for you!" she said. I was confused. I had never heard anyone refer to being a teacher as if it were charity work. We hiked through the forest to a beach. We sat on the sand and watched the crew set up picnic tables for our lunch. I told the woman that my sister was the bartender on the boat. "I think this would be a great job to have as a young person, you know, after college," she said.

I nodded. I didn't tell her that my sister hadn't been to college. And, I suspected, neither had half the crew. I knew from what Sarah had told me that many people kept the job long-term as a means to travel cheaply, sometimes moving up the chain of command to purser, or hotel manager, or first mate, but it either meant marrying someone else who worked on the boat, or a life of short-term relationships.

Later that day we had steak for dinner. I'd only had steak a few times in my life and it was delicious. "This steak is so good!" I exclaimed.

"I've had better," muttered the man sitting next to me.

I told the man I was thinking about buying some art when we got to the fishing village, but I wasn't sure what to buy.

"The thing you should do is find an artist you like and commission something," he said.

"I was thinking of, like, a poster," I said.

After dinner in the cocktail lounge my father and I chatted with Sarah at the bar. My father asked her how much the

THE END OF MY CAREER

other guests had paid for their cruise. "Oh, I think about eight thousand dollars," she said.

My father's eyes bugged out while we did the math. This meant the corporate lawyer and his family had just spent almost as much money as my parents made in a year combined.

The rest of the passengers were now gathering in the lounge. Some of the men were talking about fine whiskeys, three women exchanged anecdotes about their children's careers. Suddenly, the blurry borders of our discomfort were starting to snap into focus.

My sister got busy serving other guests and my father looked at me. "Let's go into our cabin," he said. "I want to talk to you."

"What?" I said, once inside the cabin with the door closed.

"Now remember what Sarah said about not telling anyone what we paid for our trip—"

"I know, Dad, she already told us that."

"But seriously. Eight thousand dollars! That's way more than what I was thinking. So don't tell them that Sarah is your sister either."

"But they've already seen us talking to her. Some people already know."

"Well don't advertise it. We don't want to put your sister's job at risk." My dad looked worried and his eyes darted from side to side. "*And* don't tell them I'm an electrician, tell them I'm in real estate."

I nodded. I thought my father was going overboard, but I figured I'd play along if it made him feel better. And this one was actually a lie of omission, since he did help my mother in her fledgling real estate business. It seemed innocuous not to mention the other ninety percent of how he made his living. "And don't say there are seven kids in our family," he went on, as if he were checking off a list in his head.

"*What?* What do you want me to say if someone asks? Do you just want me to lie to their faces?" Now I was imagining a fate worse than having to make small talk with wealthy retirees: maintaining an improvised lie that my father and I would construct ad hoc. Plus, even when I was telling the truth, I was sometimes inconsistent with the number of siblings I had; as a family we'd just informally adopted my friend Bekah. I'd only recently started referring to her as my sister. Sometimes I had five sisters, sometimes six. If even when I was telling the truth I sounded fishy, how was I supposed to lie?

"Just change the subject," he said and slipped out of the cabin before I could argue.

There were still five days left of the cruise. A ball of dread began to knot itself in my belly. My father began abandoning me to other tables at mealtimes. I did my best to blend in. While the other guests talked about their yachts, country clubs, sailing, and travel, while the women did laps on deck in their tracksuits and the men smoked cigars, I hung out in the lounge and attempted to read the one book I'd brought with me: *The Power of Myth* by Joseph Campbell. I was so stressed that I became totally constipated, unable to have a bowel movement in our tiny cabin, on the toilet in the shower.

Of course, it was probably pointless, this attempt to pass ourselves off as wealthy, or at least in the same class of people who might remotely be able to afford this trip; our cheap clothes, our propensity for emotional openness and self-deprecation had already given us away as working class, or at least "not wealthy."

In hindsight I can only wonder at what the other guests thought of me: a young working-class girl who for the first time had a mirror stuck up to her own face. She was shocked by what she saw—her own lack of opportunities, an air of ignorance and naiveté. The guests, on the other hand, had no mirror shoved to their faces, only me, a reminder of that part of society they were privileged enough to mostly ignore.

On our way back south to Vancouver, the boat stopped in Victoria, BC, and the company treated the staff (my father and I tagged along at Sarah's insistence) to high tea at the Empress hotel, a treat we never would have been able to afford on our own. After nearly a week of stuffing myself with croissants, steaks, and fresh pineapple, the three-tiered sandwich tray looked almost insurmountable. My stomach hurt and I still hadn't had a proper poop. But goldarnit, this was a special treat, and I wasn't going to miss my opportunity. So I excused myself and wandered downstairs to an out-of-the-way bathroom in the basement of the hotel. I sat on the toilet for what seemed like hours, determined to poop. Finally, I succeeded with much grunting and tears streaming down my face. After spending a week having everything done for me by the staff of the boat, this felt like a real accomplishment. I flushed, washed my hands, met the others upstairs, and ate.

On September 10, the last day of the cruise, we were dropped off on Vancouver's waterfront at an open-air market and city park. I was relieved to say goodbye to the other passengers. My father, ever his cheerful self, asked them what they were all up to next. Shopping and planning their next cruise was the general response.

As the other passengers dispersed into the market to shop, my father and I, who never shop for fun, wandered into the

Lawrence
and Marguerite

THE OWNER OF THE CHEESE SHOP was a middle-aged Chinese man named Lawrence. He also owned the building and lived above the shop. Lawrence met me on my first day at 8:00 a.m. outside the front door.

"I'm going to pay you in cash until you are through your probationary period," he said.

"Okay," I nodded. I didn't care, and truthfully I was nervous about working again after being sick, even if selling cheese was a job I'd done for five years already. This job was on probation for me as much as I was on probation for Lawrence.

Lawrence hurriedly showed me the opening procedure for the shop: Unlock the doors, price the bread delivery, and put the baguettes in the basket by the door. Turn on the lights and start unloading the fridges.

Unlike my last job at the grocery store, Lawrence kept many cheeses out on the shelves at room temperature.

"They do it this way in Europe!" he barked at me while he heaved large chunks of aged cheddar and Romano onto the wooden shelves behind the counter.

"Oh really?" I said. I knew this fact already, but what harm was it to act interested?

"Yes! I've been selling cheese for twenty-five years! This is the right way to store cheese!"

"Twenty-five years? Wow! You've owned this shop for a long time," I said, cheerful.

"Yes! Twenty-five years. So don't tell me I don't know about cheese!"

I could have said "Okay," but suddenly I wasn't sure what conversation we were having. I didn't say anything and started sweeping instead.

At noon, Marguerite, the tiny dark-haired woman who would train me, arrived and threw her canvas bag behind the counter. Marguerite was probably in her late forties and spoke with a French-sounding accent. She was beautiful and pale and very short. Now I can't remember where she was from originally. Was it Québec? Was it Belgium? She shook my hand without smiling and put on an apron and washed her hands.

Lawrence and Marguerite hardly spoke a word to each other as Lawrence retreated into the office and Marguerite began walking around the shop in a counter-clockwise direction, looking the shelves up and down, as if checking to see that we hadn't screwed anything up too badly before her arrival. She returned to the counter and glanced at the closed office door. She told me we should start to clean the cheese together.

Cleanliness is a big problem in cheese shops. This is mostly due to the fact that cheese is the congealed bodily fluid of farm animals that is aged and treated with mold. Cleanliness was always an important issue at the grocery store where I'd worked as well, but the product moved so fast that our cheese was seldom moldy or expired. But looking around, I guessed that it was probably a constant struggle in this shop. In all the hours I'd been there, there had only been three customers.

While we cleaned the rinds with vinegar and freshly laundered towels, I asked Marguerite how long she'd been working at the shop.

Marguerite told me she'd worked for Lawrence for a couple years. "But he doesn't know anything about cheese," she hissed, glancing at the office door. "I know much more than he does. He fell into this job because he bought the building. He doesn't care about cheese. How could he? He's Chinese!" She emphasized this last part with a flourish of her small, pale hand.

I just nodded. Maybe she was right, maybe Lawrence didn't know very much about cheese. Yes, I knew that cheese didn't originate in Asia, and I knew that many Asians and Africans were lactose intolerant, but hey, half of my very white family was lactose intolerant, and I knew I was probably lactose intolerant deep down too but I wouldn't admit it to myself and tried to pretend that I just had IBS so I could keep eating cheese. Did that make anyone less able to sell cheese?

Business remained slow. Marguerite showed me how to cut and wrap the cheese, and where things were stored. She told me that if it got busy, one of us would put cheeses away, while the other would take cheeses down and cut them for customers.

"It gets busy at about three or four," Marguerite told me and slid a *Vanity Fair* magazine from underneath her jacket below the cash register. She started flipping through it absentmindedly.

"When should I eat lunch?" I asked.

"I don't eat lunch usually," she said, and then looked me up and down like she thought maybe I shouldn't eat lunch either, or any food, ever. "But, if you want to eat you can take a half-hour break and sit outside."

I went outside and hurriedly ate my leftover Chinese food from the takeout box with the silverware I'd brought from home. The backyard was a jumble of palms and clover plants like many in San Francisco, and there was no covered area; I wondered where I was supposed to eat when the weather got cooler, or when it rained. My stomach hurt. I'd been constipated for days. The antidepressant I was weaning myself off was giving me weird symptoms. My whole body kind of ached. I'd already spent a good twenty minutes on the toilet before Marguerite arrived. I worried that Lawrence thought I was hiding in there.

After my lunch, there were still no customers. Marguerite was reading her magazine. I asked her what I should do. "Walk around the store and see if anything is expired," she replied, not looking up.

I wandered out into the store and perused the bottles of expensive olive oil, crackers, and vinegar. Unlike the cheese, Lawrence seemed to pick products with unbelievably long shelf lives. The wine never went bad and the crackers were dated well into the following year. I found one box of expired chocolate and brought it back to Marguerite.

"Aah, this is what I will eat!" she said and cracked the box open, took out a square, and hid the rest underneath her jacket.

"So what do you do?" she said as she munched on the chocolate.

"I'm going to grad school for creative writing."

"What do you write?"

"Nonfiction. Like, memoir."

"*I* should write a book," she said—not so much as a statement of fact, but as an assertion that if anyone in the room should be a writer, it should be her, not me.

"About what?"

"About living in Prague after the fall of communism."

"That sounds interesting!"

This was too obvious a statement for her to bother acknowledging. "You should have seen me!" she said, pointing out one toe and sweeping her arm down her body. "I have a picture of myself from the early nineties in Prague. I was a punk. We were all artists living together in this old villa. It was huge and cheap! In the picture I am wearing a floor-length green velvet cape and Doc Martens. I would wear that every day. It was my costume."

"That sounds fabulous!" I said. And I meant it. This description of herself as a young artist made Marguerite more human, likeable even. "I would love for you to bring in that photo and I could draw it," I said. I was drawing a lot back then and was feeling generous. Plus, I'd worked enough service jobs to know that if you don't make friends with your coworkers, the job will at best be bearable, and at worse, unbearable.

"Yes, I stayed until the money ran out. It was wonderful."

"I had a friend who taught English in Prague for a while. She said she gained a lot of weight from eating all the wonderful pastries all the time." I realized this was my only story about Prague.

Marguerite's lip curled in disgust. "You can get fat anywhere," she said. "Besides, Prague has changed so much … "

her voice faded away into a mist of nostalgia. "What time is it?"

She glanced at the clock. It was two o'clock. "Now I run," she said. And she proceeded to run in place behind the counter for half an hour.

I went home that night still on the fence about my job at the cheese shop. It had the potential to be a low-stress source of income, but my body hurt from standing all day and I was beginning to feel as if I were coming down with the flu. The truth was, I didn't know yet

if I was physically capable of having a job, even if it was only part time. But then there was the psychological aspect: I felt guilty not working. I had to wonder if I was just being lazy. Most of my classmates in grad school worked and some worked full time. I could survive financially without the job, but I didn't like the feeling that I was somehow coasting along, not living up to my fullest potential.

The next morning I arrived at the shop, this time to open the store by myself. Lawrence came down at 10:00 a.m. and started cleaning the cheese. The wine delivery driver arrived and Lawrence asked me to start pricing the champagne with the price gun. "What's the price?" I asked.

"There's inventory in the back. Look at those bottles for the price," he said.

I went into the back and saw some champagne, but it was

a different label. I came back out as the wine deliveryman set down the last of the wine. "There was some other champagne back there, but I didn't see this kind."

Lawrence looked from me to the deliveryman, and laughed. "I've owned this store for twenty-five years! I know it's back there!" And then he rolled his eyes and exchanged glances with the delivery driver. I didn't respond. I'd begun to notice a pattern.

Lawrence retreated into the office again when Marguerite arrived. As we cleaned the cheese, she told me about her old job on an organic farm, and her relationship with her boyfriend. He was an avid bicyclist. I started to open up to her as well. I told her about my health problems, I told her I'd gained seventy pounds from the cortisol, how this was the first job I'd had since I was sick.

I asked her if she liked this job.

"I need this job," she said, staring at me for a moment to impress the gravity of her situation, as if I wasn't being paid, and in fact was doing the job for fun.

"But it's gotten better," she said. "Lawrence and I used to fight all the time. I had to tell him to brush his teeth after eating. It was disgusting!" she sneered.

I ran my tongue over my teeth reflexively.

A wine rep came in at noon and the three of us stood over a little folding table, sampling wine with crackers and some salami Lawrence cut up for us. As we all joked and enjoyed ourselves, I decided that maybe I would hang onto this job. But then I started feeling a little dizzy and ate most of the salami. I realized that I didn't quite like the feeling of being tipsy at noon.

After the wine rep left, Lawrence muttered something about brushing his teeth and hurried into the bathroom.

He came out again and was talkative and jovial. He told me about his daughter. She was going to college on a music scholarship. When I showed interest he brought an old VHS tape out of his office and put it in the television over in the corner. "That's your daughter?" I said when I saw the teenage girl on stage. "She's great!"

"Mozart," he said.

I asked him about his childhood in China and some of the people who used to work in the shop. Apparently one of them was a writer and had written a novel with a character based on Lawrence. "He changed the name, but I knew it was me!" Lawrence grinned.

When the after-work crowd came in, the store became very busy. Lawrence and Marguerite, despite their mutual dislike, worked like a well-oiled machine. I tried to keep up even though I was still learning where the cheeses were stored. A customer asked for some pâté and I began to help him, instead of asking Lawrence, because I didn't want to hear him tell me how long he'd owned the store. I grabbed what seemed to be the right loaf of pâté and sliced it for the customer. Lawrence looked over and scowled at me. "What are you doing? Are you an idiot? That's the wrong one!" He smiled at the customer and took the pâté away from me, shoving me aside. "If you want something done right you have to do it yourself!" he said to the customer, smiling, and wrapped the piece back up and put it away.

I'd had enough experience with bosses and service jobs to know that I couldn't let this incident humiliate me. As a new employee, you are always the idiot until proven otherwise. In addition to this, his treatment of me showed that Lawrence and his business were insecure. And naturally he was just taking it out on me. This was not a new experience in my working life. It deviated from the norm only in its particularities. He was probably worried about the Whole Foods market down the street. I'd already been inside to check out their cheese section. They didn't stock as many different cheeses as Lawrence did, but everything was clean, vacuum-packed, and didn't have that ripe Brie smell, which some people are turned off by. Lawrence's shop, on the other hand, smelled very funky, had a much better selection, and had a French-sounding woman behind the counter—all measures of some imagined authenticity. Never mind that when I poked around on the internet I uncovered numerous one- and two-star Yelp reviews about the bad customer service provided by the "dark-haired French lady."

From what I could gather, Lawrence was keeping Marguerite around because he was insecure about the fact that he was a Chinese cheesemonger, even though the neighborhood patrons seemed to love him. This was an insecurity that Marguerite had picked up on, and kept alive with her slight jabs and hissing snobbishness. I could imagine myself at the job, if I stayed, becoming more and more demoralized, caught between the two in their dysfunctional dance. Plus, what was I offering? I added no authenticity to the shop and I was less experienced than either of them. Most likely I would end up being the token scapegoat, a common role in close-quartered menial service environments. No thanks.

As I feared, the pâté incident was the beginning of the end of my short career at the shop. Every subsequent shift Lawrence would either ask what was wrong with me, ask if I was an idiot, or tell me loudly and boastfully how long he'd owned the store.

Then one day Lawrence told me he'd hired a woman named Anna, from Sweden. She was a tall thin blonde with a nice smile and a thick accent. I never heard him ask her if she was an idiot. I was still being paid in cash; I guess I'd just been a placeholder until Lawrence could find a bona-fide European to replace me.

I called in sick the next weekend. I *was* sick. I felt horrible. Getting off the antidepressant had been a bad idea. I was still constipated and my body ached all over. I couldn't talk to any of my fellow grad students about quitting the job, because I already felt self-conscious about my full-ride scholarship, hadn't worked up until now, and had been sick all year, sleeping sometimes during class and taking massive amounts of Vicodin. I couldn't blame them for not wanting to hear about how hard my part-time job at a cheese shop was.

Marguerite's attitude never wavered. She continued to complain about Lawrence every chance she got. During my last day working with her, I told her I wasn't feeling well, that my energy and pain were particularly bad that day.

As if she hadn't heard me she said, "I went on a twenty-mile bike ride with Hans yesterday and then I jumped in the ocean. I swam for several miles." She made the motion like she was swimming. Then, because it was two o'clock, she started running in place.

It was mid November at this point. I couldn't imagine swimming in the ocean this time of year. "Wasn't it cold?" I asked.

Marguerite turned her head, still bobbing up and down behind the counter, and looked at me with contempt. "The cold water is good for your health," she said. "You should try it some time. It will make you feel better."

Couches

FIRST THERE WAS my grandmother Peaches' powder-blue velvet Davenport with the high back and claw-feet; she would often scold me for jumping on it or wiping my wet hands on the cushions. Each time, I was unaware that I had been doing this. I was also unaware that I needed to close my legs, cross my ankles, comb my hair, and stop burping. This wasn't a couch I could sleep on.

At home, my father was the only one who ever napped on the many couches that passed into and out of our lives, and I only recall this because it has always amazed me how easy it is for him to fall asleep in the middle of the living room with music blaring and seven kids running around.

But it wasn't until I moved back in with my parents as an adult that I formed a real relationship with one of their couches. This one was a long, mid-century, hideously flowered monster, and after my two failed pituitary surgeries, I spent a year on that couch drawing pictures of famous cowboys, Civil War generals, Native Americans, Chinese emperors, and medieval headgear from encyclopedias, and watching *The Golden Girls* on opiates. I was perturbed when in season three Blanche, Rose, and Dorothy appeared with abruptly different haircuts and outfits—less eighties, more

nineties. I was further astonished when they carried on as if nothing had happened. What the heck? *Everything* had happened. My opiate-addled self felt betrayed. So I switched to *The Wire*. I turned the closed captions on to decipher, through the haze and distraction, each mumbled word of Baltimore slang.

Not all couches are created equal. Not all couches are the same. Not all couches want you to sit on them, lay down on them your tired body, your well-earned grief. The couch that stands out to me the most during this period of illness belonged to my friend Tess. It was orange, low to the ground, and secondhand. Tess had given me a key to her apartment in the Hawthorne District so that I could come over any time and lay down on her deliciously comfortable couch and sleep. I would stop there between shifts at the grocery store, trips to the post office, and social engagements to sleep for hours. It was a dark, quiet place, where I could rest and become numb. I'd often slip out before she came home from work, leaving a note of thanks.

Once, exhausted and dehydrated from bouts of diarrhea from the experimental drug that I injected each morning and night, I fumbled through the front door to find my other friend, Lisa, bleary-eyed and waking from a nap on the couch.

"What are you doing here?" she asked, confused.

"What are you doing here?" I countered.

There were other couches and keys, of course, during that time—during my year of suspenseful illness, while I waited to see if the drug worked, while I got slightly sicker and sicker. Two acquaintances, Susanna and Aliscia, gave me the keys to their house in Ladd's Addition. There was a sectional and cable television. While one was away, the other would gossip about the roommate who was absent. I paid for my free couch by playing the house therapist.

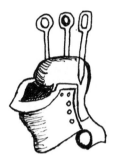

And there was my sister Bekah's place in Sellwood with the massive upholstered couch with removable pillows. I slept there almost every weekend. She and my brother-in-law pampered and fed me. I was grateful.

Over the course of that year, while I waited for the experimental drug to work, shot it into my stomach and visited the research hospital with jugs of my own urine and blood-smeared drug-log in tow, I collected keys and couches. I floated on the goodwill and pity of friends and near-strangers.

I was often alone in their houses. I preferred it that way. I wanted to be alone. I wanted to take a Vicodin, lie down on their couches, and watch daytime TV or sleep. I wanted to wrap myself in a blanket of not-feeling, to inoculate myself against despair and rage. My life, although never very goal-driven, was now in total stasis while I waited for the drug to work, while I waited for it to block the toxic cortisol as it depleted my bones, stressed my heart, corroded my brain, and made my hair fall out.

This stasis looked like sunlight falling on an empty couch in an empty house at 11:00 a.m. on a Thursday. Dust motes and *Judge Judy*.

I'd given over my life to the drug, the doctors, and my tumor. I became the reclining minor deity of The Ill. My devotees laid couches and keys at my feet. I received it as love but a part of me thought it might be an act of fear—a hedging of bets lest they too were struck down. I was, as a professor later told me, a sacred monster.

I enjoyed it. That's something I've never told anyone. That year was one of the best years of my life.

The Women's Studies Major

I. SIX SISTERS

My oldest sister is living with us while she gets a divorce.

When I was a kid, my mother told me that she felt the Kobe earthquake in her sleep from her bed in Oregon. A slight tremor woke her up in the middle of the night. She didn't know what it was. But in the morning we all watched the news.

She also said she heard the egg hit the side of the house at 4:00 a.m. a few days ago. The next morning she found the shards of shell and yellow slime on the brick and grass.

My mother regularly has dreams where she is searching for a baby. Sometimes it's my sister Rachael. Sometimes it's me. Sometimes it's just an unnamed baby.

My worst fear is that I will wake up one night to the hypnagogic jerking of my body falling from the primordial tree and I will know inexplicably that one of my six sisters has just been murdered by an ex-lover.

Our bodies connected like tree roots. I smell warnings in the wind.

We grew up jealous of each other. We grew up in love with each other.

We grew up comparing hair color, stomachs, periods, eyes, toes, lovers.

One Christmas afternoon, my sisters Zoe and Simone and I tried to make a list of all the sisters' past and present lovers on the back of an envelope, but my father made us stop.

"I can't listen to this," he said and held up a hand.

These men come and go from celebrations. One of us is always showing off for someone. I could make a pie graph of us, single, dating, and married and it would shift year to year, month to month. Some of us have been in one wedge for years.

Frequently unhappily.

Years later my father's real opinion about the lovers will surface. I want to shake him. Care more! I want to say.

My mother will fall in love and grieve every one of them openly. I want to shake her. Care less! I want to say.

I didn't know he owned guns until I'd been living with him for several months. He told me—his head on my chest as we lay in his bed—that years ago he'd been so depressed he'd gotten rid of all his bullets.

I asked him if he thought he'd ever get that depressed again.

"No. Now I have you," he said.

This was a terrible answer.

My sister, now in the throes of her divorce, tells me that the unconscious is given too much credit. That these confessions are tools—not gifts, but manipulation. A truth to use against you later.

I told you I was a thief.
I told you I was a cheater.
I told you I couldn't live without you.

We're sure it wasn't her soon-to-be-ex-husband who threw the egg at our house. Of course it wasn't, but we can't help but feel that we are under attack.

Far away there are earthquakes. Far away a baby is misplaced.

Our roots send messages. We gather together.

2. SECRETS

All of my lovers have laid their terrible secrets at my feet: the unspeakable, the silly, the troubling, the everyday theft, the habitual cheating, the despair, that time with their father's friend, the credit card debt, coke deals at the bowling alley, the accident, their specific shameful desires.

Can I trust you? was one question. *Will you love me?* was another.

Without fail I have offered up love in return. I thought it was intimacy. Even if my shameful secret was that sometimes I really didn't want their shameful secrets.

My body is nothing in comparison to these confessions. I had no agency in it: the scars, the hair loss, and whatever else.

Taking off my clothes.

My actual secrets are really secrets.

Any secret you tell is not a secret.

Most of my lovers have told me I was wholesome or innocent. It bothers me. Is it my fault that I come from a happy family? I'm not attracted to wholesome men. Apparently.

He was abused. He was neglected. His parents didn't love him or each other.

He needed us.

Oh, the ego. That we can balm the childhood. That we are sages smudging demons away.

Or maybe they didn't know me. Didn't know that yes, I would eventually leave.

Six months after we break up we meet at a coffee shop and he gives me back my drawings. I tell him that I know it was very hard for him to break up with me, and tears well up in our eyes. He reaches across the table for my hand.

"We all love you," I tell him. "My family always loved you."

He starts to cry. I put my arms around him and he shakes, sobbing in my arms.

He tells me that he is seeing someone new. They're keeping it casual. He tells me he burned my name on an altar at some kind of African grief ceremony.

I want to tell him that Africa is a big place.

I go to the store and buy a pack of cigarettes, smoke three end to end and throw the rest out the window of my car.

3. LEAVING

I've only known this man for five days and I am lying in his bed and he is pretending he is sleeping. Maybe he is pretending he is dead. I don't know. I feel alone and horny. I feel disgusting and dejected.

Get up Martha, I say to myself. *Put on your clothes and leave. It's that easy. You haven't done this since you were twenty-seven. Since before you were sick. You have to start being the one to walk away first.* I feel his confessions weighing on me.

But I heave them off, get up, and pull on my dress and underwear.

"I'm leaving, I can't do this," I say.

He grabs my hand and makes a half-hearted attempt to talk me into staying but we both know we've already ruined everything.

"I just need more affection," I say.

It feels like a secret, but it's only partly true.

I can't even tell the whole truth.

I drive aimlessly through his neighborhood. I finally hit Stark Street, get my bearings, and start towards home.

I need love, I wordlessly think.

"There, I said it," I say out loud.

I need love.

It's not a secret anymore.

4. MY FAVORITE SONG

I go on a date with a recently divorced man. He looks like an ex-boyfriend of mine. During dinner he keeps stroking his face and yawning. He asks me what kind of music I like and replies in a barely concealed monotone. "Oh, really. Uh huh."

The band plays a folky version of "No Diggity" and we dance. He tells me I have some great moves and I say thanks.

He never mentions his ex-wife. At my car, I ask to kiss him but later it makes me sick that I was asking him for anything. I pull into a convenience store and buy a pack of cigarettes. I take one out and give the rest to a homeless woman sitting on the curb outside.

5. SELFIES

I am sitting on the toilet thinking about myself at age sixteen, clutching the steering wheel of my Subaru Justy, idling at a stoplight in Gresham, Oregon. I don't look at the car next to me. The energy from the next car burns at me. I know they are staring.

I'd learned to look straight ahead, to keep my head down. I'd learned that men at stoplights, from the safety of their cars in the summertime, with the windows rolled down, in the mid-nineties in Gresham, make obscene gestures and rev their engines at young girls. At me.

The gestures were an act of violence, more or less.

This wasn't covered at the DMV. It wasn't part of my training. I was taught how to yield, to follow the rules.

And so I took to taking every compliment as an act of violence. I could not discern between the two: eye contact and a smile. I will kill you. Please acknowledge me. You are nothing.

Avoidance of pain is more powerful than the pursuit of goals. A kiss. Safety. Love. Self-regard. If you are not ready for the answer, don't ask the question: *If the whole world wants to fuck me, why don't you love me?*

I ask myself: *Who needs the validation of others?* You have to love yourself first and other garbage, other waste to process, excreting the unusable.

Perhaps the last to go is anger. I stand up, flush. I let myself fantasize.

About taking my imagined Justy of old and ramming it into those men, their eyes growing round with fright, the tables deliciously turning. I think of them abandoning their cars, fleeing in terror. I imagine chasing them through the streets with a baseball bat and what? Violence. I think about how strong my legs might have been and how weak my arms may have been.

But then, as always goes with these fantasies, I imagine them turning and beating me until I am dead.

Just like you would to anyone who had frightened you, right?

I feel overfed, nauseous on violence. What pleasure is it to strike something smaller than yourself?

I wash my hands.

But now, at least in this aspect, it's much better: I am beautiful, even to myself.

I take selfies. I post pictures of my breasts on the internet. I have taken to locking my apartment door and walking around naked behind the gauzy curtains.

Some dating expert on a video tells me he's turned off by too many selfies. Whatever. He should be grateful to have a moment of peace from his constant arousal.

I come from abundance. My heart is opening. My skin is clear. I stand up straight and look men in the eye. I smile.

And I'm doing push-ups every day.

6. LINK

I ask my father to read an article about male entitlement and emotional labor.

"Can you just tell me what it says?" he says.

7. MARRIAGE MATERIAL

I haven't spoken to my father since our argument. I've been reading about abuse, emotional labor. I'm reading a book, *All the Single Ladies*. Maybe I don't want to get married. Maybe I am actually okay not being in a relationship. Maybe I don't want to be monogamous. Maybe I'll never cohabitate again. I have nieces and nephews; maybe I don't need to have kids. Maybe my female friendships and my relationships with my sisters will end up being the most important relationships of my life.

8. THE MORNING WITHOUT MEN

I get up and get dressed. I put on my headphones and turn my Pandora station to Adele. As the rain breaks and the sun comes out, I walk down to the park and "Chasing Pavements" comes on.

I see one man way off on the soccer field and another woman walking her dog. *Who cares?* I think, and I scream/sing as loudly as I can, jogging down the path.

And the idea flashes across my brain: I decide that I will no longer support men. I will not support their egos, or their projects. I will not care if they like me. I will not listen to them. I will not care about their problems. I will only offer simple half-baked solutions when they bring up their interpersonal problems. I will say, "Just break up with her." I will say, "Just tell him you don't like that."

I feel my heart exploding with possibilities. It's only women from today on out. For one year. It will be my "Year Without Men." I will write a book about it. It will be a bestseller, like that Zero Carbon Man. I will act as many men I know: I will not support male anything, unless it's in a sexual manner. They have their arena and I have mine. If anyone asks why I only work for women, I will just shrug and say it wasn't on purpose, it just "ended up that way." If someone accuses me of hating men, I'll just smile and say, "Are you kidding? I love my dad! And I love dick!"

But then I think of some of my male friends. I decide that I will make an exception for men of color and gay men. And my male family members. And my publisher. And Leonard. What about if a man refers me business, will I return the favor? I frown. Maybe I will have to think about this a little bit more.

A woman walks by me on the trail and I smile at her so big she looks at me weird.

It's not that I want to be like a man. I'm just not sure I want to be a woman anymore, in the way that I was.

A song comes on. For a second I think it's "No Diggity." But it's "Grandma's Hands" by Bill Withers. I love Bill Withers.

I check my phone for text messages.

I'm looking forward to my next date with the man with the traumatic brain injury, the PTSD, the war vet, the one who is kind of a dreamboat, the one who is an excellent kisser and has a degree in women's studies, the one with the knuckle and neck tattoos, the one who I want to fuck, that one.

I have given up on my book idea by the time I get home.

9. WE ALL WANT TO FEEL SAFE

I would never have gone on a date with him if I hadn't seen on his profile that he had a degree in women's studies.

He notices the medical alert dog tag around my neck immediately. I tell him about my missing adrenal glands and Cushing's Disease. He tells me about being a drummer in a metal band.

He makes cute jokes at his own expense.

He tells me that his ex-wife had been a drug addict. And much older than him—that she had told him to marry her and join the Army. He was shipped off to Iraq. He tells me he and his son are very close.

He tells me he has PTSD from the war. I tell him I also have mild PTSD from having had Cushing's Disease probably since when I was in utero.

He tells me if you aren't working on yourself, getting therapy, that's a deal-breaker.

I tell him my last therapist traumatized me.

"I'm sorry that happened to you," he says.

I tell him I'll give him some of the pot cookies I've made.

"I guess that means we are going to see each other again," he says.

He reaches across the table and grabs my hand. It's decisive. And attractive.

When we kiss I feel a sigh of relief. He backs away and puts his hands on his head. "Oh my god!"

"Are you okay?" I giggle.

"I haven't been kissed like that in years," he says.

A week passes. The Women's Studies Major texts me. He tells me he isn't ready to get involved with me. Or anyone.

I go on more bad dates. Everyone is named the same name as my dad, which is also my brother's name. One guy I have been messaging, I find out later, likes to dress up like a pirate regularly. I can't sleep with someone who dresses up like a pirate. Another one is so sour-faced and negative I leave before we even get our drinks. Another man keeps interrupting me and arguing with me. After our date I shiver and shake all the way home, exhausted and confused. When I get home I find a yoga video on YouTube and yawn and stretch for an hour.

I go on a date with someone who kisses me very badly. I can't understand why he even bothered.

I can't stop thinking about the Women's Studies Major. I text him and ask him if we can be friends. If we can be Facebook friends.

He agrees.

10. I'M SORRY THAT HAPPENED TO YOU

I end up un-friending one of the men I've dated on Facebook because he tells me another woman accused him of rape. I ask him why he thinks this keeps happening to him. He tells me that it's more common than I think. He tells me that he is secretly eating meat and none of his vegan friends know. I ask him why he suddenly started eating meat and drinking alcohol again after being a vegan straight edge for more than five years.

"I was finally cured of hepatitis," he says.

We had had sex with a condom. Thank god. But I still feel sick.

"Your life is like a horror movie," I say, not caring that I am being mean.

He looks hurt. "Your life is like a body horror movie," he says.

"Is that a genre?"

"Yes, it's like *The Fly*."

"Yeah, I have often thought that. Like *The Metamorphosis*," I say. "Like Kafka."

He frowns like he doesn't know what I am referencing and because he meant to hurt me and I don't seem hurt.

11. METAMORPHOSIS

My body is changing. I am on estrogen and progesterone. I am working out every day. My legs lose all their fat. My waist is becoming defined. Sometimes in planks and downward dogs I look at my little belly, hanging there, with affection. It's cute. My hair is getting thick and curly. I start taking Wellbutrin. I cry because everything seems so beautiful. Because I finally feel safe in my body. Because my voice is getting stronger and louder. I orgasm more easily. I drive faster. I smell and taste and feel things as being more intense, sensual, delicious. I feel like I'm high, but then I think maybe this is just what being healthy feels like. And then I get sad because I have missed so much. I have spent so many years as a larva.

I buy a cherry red Honda Coupe. It has a sunroof.

The Women's Studies Major texts me and tells me that all my adventures on Facebook make him want to go on them with me.

My plan is working then, I reply.

We go down to my secret spot on the river and make out. He is strong. It feels good to let him move my body into different positions. He kisses my neck. I nearly come in his arms. We half jokingly talk about going into the bushes and having sex, but I tell him I don't want to. I lie on my back and he runs his fingers over my breasts and stomach.

"Do you see all my scars?" I ask.

He nods. "I wasn't going to say anything. It's your story."

We kiss some more, I put my hands on his face but he won't open his eyes. "You're avoiding eye contact," I say.

"The sun," he says.

It's not that bright, I think.

We lie next to each other in silence in the warm sand. We hold hands, he takes my hand and kisses it. I smile because it reminds me of something I would do and then feel silly and vulnerable about later.

He tells me it's hard to maintain your humanity when you've been trained to kill. And tells me about his father. About growing up with an absent mother. He tells me about his uncle who grabbed his hand and turned it over, telling him that his hands were too soft.

"Sounds like toxic masculinity," I say.

"It's all toxic," he mutters.

12. LOVE LANGUAGE

I am still not really speaking to my father because he still refuses to read the article. We have a big fight. I tell him that if he would just read the article, he would realize how ridiculous he is being.

"You keep saying, 'Read the article, read the article' …. What is it about?"

I storm out of the room and then several days later we pretend like nothing happened.

13. ONE OF THE GOOD ONES

The Women's Studies Major texts me and tells me he is sorry to hear about my friend who died, and how am I doing?

We make plans for me to spend the night at his new place that Saturday. He tells me that it can be a nonsexual sleepover.

Before we meet up I have dinner with my friends Kate and Mark. I officiated their wedding. They met on OkCupid several years ago.

Mark says he has never met someone with the Women's Studies Major's name who hasn't been a douche bag.

"I know! He's a women's studies major though!"

Mark laughs, "That can be either good or really bad."

"He's one of the good ones," I say.

Later that night I follow the Women's Studies Major to his new place. He's just moved in, his son is at his mom's house. The small house is dark and stacked with boxes. A huge canister of Muscle Milk sits on the counter by the refrigerator.

I take off my clothes while he is out of the room, crawl into his bed. There is nothing in the room but his bed, a nightstand, and some boxes.

He undresses and gets under the covers with me. He begins to touch me all over my body, bending over me and kissing my stomach, caressing me. It feels natural and good.

"Can I take these off?"

"Yes," I say. He pulls down my underwear and asks me if he can go down on me.

"I'm not ready for that," I say. "It's too intimate. Will you touch me?"

We touch each other.

I put his penis in my mouth and touch myself. He keeps telling me how good it feels. I have no trouble coming.

"Do you want to have sex?" I ask. "I don't want to pressure you. I know you just got out of a relationship."

"Oh, I'm ready," he says, smiling.

Then. "By the way, I had a vasectomy."

I laugh. "Do you have a condom?"

When we fuck it hurts.

We lay in bed talking and he strokes my back. He thanks me. He says he needed that. We talk about growing up poor. I ask him what his favorites movies are. He tells me he likes comedies. "I can't watch violent movies, or movies with rape in them."

I tell him my favorite movie is *Raising Arizona*. He tells me he loves that movie and we exchange lines from the film and giggle. He falls asleep, his body jerking every so often. I don't sleep hardly at all. My body keeps relaxing and jerking itself awake.

In the morning he pulls me to him and runs his hands up my chest, over my breasts, around my neck. I turn over and we start kissing, I gently bite him, we tease each other, pulling our mouths away, feeling tongues, necks, he puts his mouth on my nipples. When we fuck I grab his ass, I put my legs behind his shoulders, I feel strong.

"I thought you weren't a morning person," he teases me.

He tells me he used to run around with a group of "thugs" that would beat up skinheads. Anti-racist punks. I tell him I know about the racism problem in Oregon. "This town is crawling with Nazis," he says.

It all went south when one of his friends was shot by a Nazi and ended up in a wheelchair.

"We didn't want to get the cops involved," he says. "We never got the guy that did it though."

"Do you regret that decision?"

"I don't hang out with those guys anymore."

"Why do you think you were drawn to that?"

He looks exhausted by the question and lets out a sigh.

I giggle, "You're going to have to get used to this. I ask a lot of questions."

He looks at the ceiling. "I have a lot of training. I thought I could keep people from getting into trouble."

When I leave I notice the baseball bat by the door.

14. HORSE MEAT

A couple days later I text him late at night about the dinner we are going to have on Saturday and how I am thinking about his dick in my mouth.

He has been texting me every day. I almost go to Ikea with him to pick up new furniture for his house but decide against it because it seems too relationshippy. Talking about dicks over text is fine.

But Ikea and dicks do make me think about meatballs. I ask him if he wants meatballs for dinner on Saturday.

"Fuck yeah," he texts.

15. HAPPY VALLEY

I am cat-sitting out in Happy Valley. I am happy to be away from our crowded duplex, my parents, my sister Ana and her kids coming and going on the other side of my wall.

After I work out, I go upstairs into the large room where I am staying and look out the large windows at the rolling hills covered in trees and enormous houses. They seem to go on forever. It's weird out here. This house is probably at least six thousand square feet. The room I am staying in has a bathroom with skylights in it, a tiled shower with a glass door.

It's another world and I feel different here. Since I have been staying in Happy Valley, I've had my nails done. My new shiny red car doesn't look out of place in the driveway. I went to Nordstrom and Victoria's Secret. I was afraid my boobs had shrunk since working out, but the woman in the dressing room tells me they are still a D-cup, which is thrilling to me. I buy underwear and a new bra. A sign in the Victoria's Secret window says "No padding is hot now" over a picture of a flat-chested model in a swimsuit.

Fuck that, I think. *Just when I finally get boobs they are going out of style. Fuck you telling me what's hot.*

I remember Carl Brown telling me I was flat-chested when I was twelve. I remember the boys in middle school snapping our bras.

My mom is unimpressed when I tell her later about how big my boobs still are.

"This is a big deal for me, Mom, you don't understand."

She gets up and closes the door to her office so the secretary can't hear us talk about my boobs.

I turn on the Alicia Keys station and take a shower and watch myself in the mirror. I notice how beautiful my body looks, the muscles in my legs, my ass, my breasts. I imagine the Women's Studies Major and myself having sex in the shower and fucking in the huge bed in the other room.

When I was twenty-five I dated an older man. One day he stood in the doorway and watched me shower.

"What are you doing?" I asked.

"Just watching you," he said.

"Well, you're creeping me out."

16. MY MC NAME IS CHRONICALLY ILL

I have a grower out in Tillamook who gives me butter and oil and lots of weed. I make pans of cookies, wrap them up in green plastic wrap, and stack them in my freezer. After I give one to my friend Casey, he sends me a text of an emoji rainbow skull melting. "One bite," he texts.

I don't generally like being high. It makes me panicky and paranoid. Even without adrenals.

I use a vape pen most of the time. I like a strain called Girl Scout Cookies.

I'm not feeling good this week. My mother and I have both had intestinal issues. Bouts of diarrhea leave me feeling exhausted. I decide to take a nap in bed with my laptop and vape pen alongside me.

I look all over the place for the charger to my vape pen but can't find it. I must have left it back at my apartment in Gresham. I take one of the pot cookies out of the freezer and set it on the granite countertop at the house in Happy Valley. I take a butter knife and shave the tiniest corner off the cookie and eat it along with some dinner. I turn on the TV and start watching the end of the Sanders-Clinton debate. I don't feel anything so I go back to the kitchen and break off a tiny bit more of the cookie.

When I start giggling over a pretzel commercial I know the cookie is starting to kick in. I get on Facebook and get into a conversation with my sister Zoe in New Orleans. I send her a link to the pretzel commercial.

"This is hysterical," I type.

"I'm a little stoned," I type.

She sends me a link to a viral video about a woman whose two older brothers tricked her into thinking it's the zombie apocalypse. I can't stop laughing about it. But then I find a clip of them being interviewed on *The Ellen Degeneres Show* and I begin to wonder if they are lying and have made the whole thing up. The video is just too edited, plus who would be so gullible as to think it was the zombie apocalypse?

"I think they are lying," I type to Zoe.

17. ALL THE MONSTERS

Once when I was babysitting my neighbor's kids, I read them *Hansel and Gretel*. After I was done reading it to them I asked Marcel what the scariest part was. Was it the witch? Was it when Hansel was put in a cage so he could be fattened up?

No, Marcel said. It was when their father left them in the woods alone.

But I was never scared of being alone. I like being alone. I was always scared of the devil, of underwater dinosaurs, witches. All the monsters lurking in the dark.

18. E-PRIME

I am way too high.

I think about Saturday, the Women's Studies Major coming over. How he is texting me every day. The sexy outfit I have picked out. Maybe it's too sexy. Maybe this is all about sex. Maybe I shouldn't lead with sex.

I hate this. This always happens when I get too high. I get paranoid and my heart races. It reminds me of being sick and anxious all the time.

Does anyone know that he is coming over here? I'm all alone out here in this huge house. What do I actually know about the Women's Studies Major? He has already told me that he went around beating up Nazis for fun. And he has a teenage son. That's totally irresponsible. What is this anyway, are we suddenly in a relationship? I've already told him I am going to see other people. I told him I don't want to jump into anything. He said he doesn't want to either. He said what I do on my own time is none of his business.

And yet he is texting me every day.

It's dark now. And my hands and the tip of my nose are going cold. I put on several layers and crawl into bed. I pull my laptop up onto the blankets and go to YouTube. I watch a TED Talk about beauty. The speaker is a beautiful black woman. She describes beauty as being a racialized concept. And that it excludes the disabled and the fat. It excludes a lot of people. I think about my own blond hair and blue eyes. I think about how I used to be fat and now still have problems with body image. I think about how we should say

"I find you beautiful" instead of "You are beautiful." Beauty is in the eye of the beholder, after all. And our language colonizes all it touches. The verb "to be" colonizes the known world. It gives the speaker a false and unearned objectivity. My friend Peter used to talk a lot about E-Prime, a form of English where there is no "to be." I think he used to challenge himself to write only in E-Prime so as not to colonize the world, so that his subjectivity was acknowledged. I think about all of this and know I am still too high to sleep. The video comes to an end.

I think, *What harm is it to Google the Women's Studies Major?*

19. THE GIFT OF FEAR

When I was in middle school, my father once had a traveling salesperson come into his real estate office selling mace. He told us about it that night, recounting some of the scary statistics about violence against women the man shared in his sales pitch. He had purchased one can of mace, in a little leather pouch on a key ring. He gave it to my mother. Mostly I remember the fear in my father's face, and then the feeling I had, the feeling of embarrassment that he should have already known all those scary statistics—that women are in danger. I know I knew. All I had to do was watch TV.

20. TOO HIGH

A WordPress page with his name in the address pops up. I click on the link.

At first I can't really absorb what I'm looking at. The page recounts an incident in 2003 when the Women's Studies Major hit his wife in the head, kicked her in the back, threatened to kill her, and was charged with menacing and assault in the fourth degree.

My heart starts to race as I scroll down.

The narrative continues with the Women's Studies Major's own testimony about the abuse he inflicted on his wife. He was forced to go through a diversionary program for abusers and apparently was forced to write this account as part of the program. He admits to physically threatening his wife at the time, trying to control her, emotional manipulation, throwing things at her, pushing her, kicking her, and a long list of emotional and physical abuse. He admits to using male privilege to insult and control his wife and other women in his life.

The website was put together by the friend of a woman who was in a relationship with the Women's Studies Major in 2011 and was also abused by him. He choked her and did all manner of things to her including threatening to kill her pets. The friend put up the website to warn other women.

I feel like my eyes are crossing. I check back and forth from Google to the website. How high am I? Is this right? I feel suddenly very alone. All alone. And in the dark. I close the blinds and crawl back into bed.

I call my mom.

21. FREAKING OUT

"Oh my god, Mom, I am so glad you're still awake!" I say. "First off, I just want to tell you that I am very high."

"Okay …."

"I ate too much of one of my pot cookies and then I found out the guy that I have been seeing is an ABUSER AND THREATENED TO KILL HIS WIFE!!"

"Wait, what?"

"I looked him up on the internet and he has been arrested for domestic abuse. He's a total abuser!"

"He is abusive?"

I hear my sister in the background. "Ana wants to talk to you." She hands the phone to my sister.

Ana and I have a long conversation and I tell her all about it. Until the end of the conversation, I am too high to realize that she is mostly placating me and just thinks I am totally high and catastrophizing.

We hang up forty-five minutes later.

I text my friend Ledena and we text back and forth for half an hour. I tell her I am going to confront him in the morning and tell him I don't want to see him anymore. She says she doesn't know if that is a good idea. I send an email to all my closest friends telling them how scared I am and how I have to stay out here in Happy Valley two more nights and am FREAKING OUT. And would someone come out to stay with me?

I deactivate my Facebook account. I deactivate my Ok-Cupid account. I make my Instagram private. I block the two men who started following my selfies on Instagram

81

from my Tinder profile even though I never swiped right on them because one of them is creepy and in an open relationship and the other one is a short guy who works at a grocery store and is too old.

I don't sleep all night.

22. MEDICAL MARIJUANA SAVES LIVES

I get a text in the morning from Ana: "Holy shit."

I'd sent her a link to the website and she's just now reading it.

My friend Aisha calls me. She tells me it's very unlikely that he will do anything. She doesn't think I should tell him I know about the website.

"Dudes do it all the time," she says. "Just cancel your date for tomorrow, tell him you're sick. If he texts, respond very neutrally. A few days later if he keeps texting, make up some bullshit thing about how you have to focus on yourself."

I nod. I'm staring at the floor in the living room waiting for my mom to come over. I feel like I can't sleep unless I know someone is here with me. I have just taken my morning dose of hydrocortisone and I feel insane.

"Look, I realize that he probably won't do anything, but I have PTSD from my Cushing's Disease!" My voice starts to crack. "I catastrophize. That's what I do, I can't help it! Plus I found out all of this because I got high and paranoid. I wouldn't have even Googled him if I hadn't gotten way too high!"

"Oh honey … " Aisha laughs. "You don't have to confront him for the sisterhood," she says. "You have to stay safe for the sisterhood."

23. THE SISTERHOOD

I spend the next two hours on the phone. I call Kate, I call Ann Marie, I call Sarah, I call Michael, I call Lisa, I call Jessie, I call Cat, I call Kezia, I call Taya, and I call Ledena. I feel loved but I also feel hysterical. My mom arrives and makes me get off the phone. She gives me some Benadryl and tells me to go get some rest already.

As I drift off into sleep, I stare at the open closet door. My dresses hanging in a row, my bras in a jumble on the dresser. I feel confused. I wonder if somehow I conjured the Women's Studies Major into existence. I can't see his face, like a painting that's been defaced, a pharaoh with his eyes jagged out. What's left are facts: tattoos, traumas, degrees, stories. Not a person. Just a collection of half-truths swirling around fear.

The exhaustion and Benadryl take over and then I'm asleep, dreaming of my sisters. We're running in the grass. Sarah is asking me what I need. We can't find Rachael.

I wake up. It's 5:00 p.m.

24. WHO I THOUGHT HE WAS

Claudette comes out to stay the night with me.

We make dinner together and talk about abuse, the police. Violence.

"Our culture doesn't care about women's lives," Claudette says.

She assures me that the Women's Studies Major won't do anything. "Abusers are, at heart, very insecure. He wants to make sure you won't leave him before he tries to do anything. You're not invested enough yet. You're not in love with him."

"It's just so weird," I say. "He's a total sociopath. But, the funny thing is, he really is a women's studies major! That wasn't a lie."

"The scariest thing," Claudette says, "is that someone you thought you knew isn't at all who you thought they were."

25. BUT HE WAS A NEUROSURGEON!

I know a woman who was raped by someone she met on Ok-Cupid. I know a woman who almost married a guy she met on OkCupid, who then went on to murder his wife and kill himself. He was a neurosurgeon.

I start reading about emotional abuse. I realize at some level I have been emotionally abusive to my father. It's not his fault he's triggering me. The way I feel is not his responsibility.

I find some therapists who deal with trauma and start making phone calls.

The Women's Studies Major texts me and says he doesn't know what he did to drive me away. I text him not to worry about it and to take care.

26. BACK HOME

When I get home the next day I go over to my mom and dad's side of the duplex and we chat for a while. I look out the window.

"What is that?" I ask.

There is a white smear all over the living room window.

"Someone threw another egg at our house last night," my mom says.

27. THE EXPERTS

One Dating Expert tells men not to chase women, because men who chase women are unattractive to high value females. That's beta behavior, says the Dating Expert. The Dating Expert tells women not to chase men. That's masculine behavior, says the Dating Expert. You are trying to make things happen—that's a male's role, that's masculine and will emasculate men.

Another Dating Expert tells me to get in touch with my submissive side, my feminine side. The Dating Expert tells me to channel my inner goddess. The Dating Expert tells me to spend time trying to look nice before a date so I feel confident, but not so much time that I begin to feel insecure. The Dating Expert tells me to love my life, to have a life, to not play games but to have a life. The Dating Expert tells me to pick a different part of my body to love every day.

The Dating Expert tells men to go to the mall and ask one hundred women for their numbers. The Dating Expert tells men not to be pussies. The Dating Expert tells men that women have seen a million men like them. The Dating Expert tells men to be patient, to create a fun date and an opportunity for sex to happen. The Dating Expert tells men to walk women to the car, to the door.

The Dating Expert says if I have a problem with men, the problem is me.

The Dating Expert tells me not to text back right away. The Dating Expert tells me to keep my options open. The Dating Expert tells me not to sleep with multiple men at the same time.

The Dating Expert tells men that he has slept with hundreds of beautiful, high value females. The Dating Expert talks about how she met her husband. She tells women to stop looking and they will find their soul mate. She tells women to never give up. The Dating Expert tells me to click on the link in the video for a free webinar.

The Dating Expert tells me about the three signs that a man is in love with me, the four signs that a man only wants sex, the ten lies that men tell, the seven ways that I can make a man adore me, love me, commit to me, the three signs that he is not ready for a relationship, the three signs that I am not ready for a relationship. The Dating Expert tells me to get in touch with and truly feel the pain and sadness that I have inflicted on myself for allowing myself to be treated as less than the beautiful amazing goddess that I am.

1. THE RIGHT CLOTHES

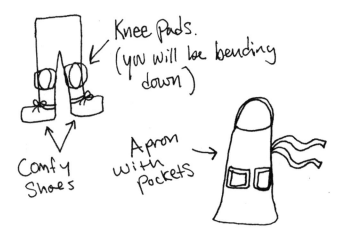

Knee Pads.
(you will be bending down)

Comfy Shoes

Apron with Pockets →

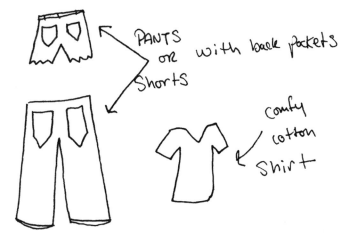

PANTS or Shorts with back pockets

comfy cotton Shirt

2. THE RIGHT TOOLS

Scraper tool

A Good ← Vacuum.

↗ Feather Duster

← Tooth Brush

Sponge →

← Lots of towels!

High Protein, healthy Snacks

Spray bottles of bleach Cleaner + General Cleaner.

Broom + MOP

Onshore Hospitality

My sister Sarah called me one day and asked if I wanted a part-time job with a local cruise company, one very similar to her former employer. The position would require sitting in a hospitality suite at a waterfront hotel on the Willamette River from 8:00 a.m. to 5:00 p.m., tagging bags and ensuring that guests got their proper transports to either the airport or the cruise ship. Basically I was to sit in a room with old, white, wealthy people for nine hours each weekend and talk to them while they waited to go somewhere else. It paid well. I said yes.

I had notions of what the passengers would be like from my experience ten years earlier on the cruise to Canada with my father. I expected them to be unbearable—unbearable, that is, without the twenty dollars an hour I was being paid to bear them.

It would also be the first time I'd work a full eight-hour shift since my stint back behind the cheese counter, so I was a little nervous; I decided to take extra steroids just to be sure I could make it through the day without any pain. Something I discovered, though, is that when not being used to fight illness, a little extra cortisol often makes me sweaty and overly chatty. As it turned out, this was a good thing in the context of the cruise job; my mission was to be friendly, act like I cared, and answer questions.

That first day on the job, with a good breakfast and a few extra steroid pills under my belt, I put on my blue button-up shirt and nametag, and headed down to the hotel. I set up a poster board with the company's name and logo outside the door to our conference room and sat down at a little table inside the door with pens, the guest itinerary, and my purse. I poured myself a cup of coffee.

The guests arrived in small groups with their luggage in tow and I checked them off the itinerary and tagged their bags with their cabin numbers. Soon I made friends with my first guest—a retired cop and weapons consultant to Hollywood (*Miami Vice* included). He'd worked in Miami his entire career and we

talked for nearly two hours about the drug wars of the '80s. He told me stories of high-speed chases in powerboats, drug heists, and corrupt cops.

The other guests were surprisingly jovial and friendly. The ladies were sweet and the men enjoyed telling me about their careers. Driving home that day, I thought about my initial apprehension that the guests would make me feel uncomfortable. I was surprised by how interesting and pleasant the guests had been; I hadn't been uncomfortable at all. Their wealth didn't intimidate or shock me in the least. Perhaps the passengers had fundamentally changed in the last ten years. Or perhaps it was me.

Of course, many of them treated me in that way that people used to being served treat service workers: with meticulous politeness, disinterest, and a kind of tired resignation to the roles that society has thrust upon all of us. It was mostly the men who treated me this way—older men on the cruise with their wives who really didn't want to go in the first place. They'd much rather be home spending their well-earned retirement doing what they'd waited their whole working lives to do: write their epic science fiction novel. (I met at least three male passengers over the course of my employment who were using their retirement to write genre fiction.) These men, and sometimes women, didn't smile at me very much; they didn't pretend to be my friend. *I'm doing my job by taking my wife on this cruise*, they seemed to suggest, *so please do yours*. They weren't interested in me as a person in the slightest. They just wanted to treat me as another private in their vacation army, both of us stoic and uncomplaining.

But some passengers were, in fact, horrible. One woman talked about the bacterial infection she believed she'd caught from all the dirty Mexicans at her neighborhood Walmart. She was very angry; she'd almost died. Another man, when the subject of family holidays came up, told me with glee, "My daughter is a liberal. I love making her cry!" Another angrily refused to leave the hotel in order to arrive at the airport early. Then, as if on cue, his elderly parents and sister surrounded me in a full circle and began to also yell at me from each of the cardinal directions about the various slights and bad service they'd received during the cruise, all the while interrupting one another and me. Luckily the family had made enemies with the other passengers during their week on the boat, and a kindly passenger came to my defense and broke up the circle of yelling adults. Eventually the family calmed down and seemed to wilt into the hotel chairs like lumpy flowers, sodden and dazed from a week of cruise ship food and booze.

Then that afternoon, two sweet old lady passengers ushered me into the hallway and told me in hushed tones how awful the family had been, how they'd been "hardcore alcoholics," how I shouldn't worry about them and all those awful things they said, and that the cruise company and I had done a fabulous job and had provided fabulous customer service.

Although the hallway encouragements warmed my heart, I chuckled to myself later about how they were concerned that I not take the family's criticisms of the service they'd received *personally*. They didn't seem to realize that, while the incident had briefly violated my sense of self and general human politeness, any ownership I took over the company, the service, etc., was beyond the scope of my pay scale to embrace in any meaningful way. Even though I had apologized and acted concerned, I did not and would not actually take responsibility for their experience while on the boat. I've worked in service my entire life and have never been the type to take responsibility for anything beyond my own actions. I know that taking personal responsibility for a company as a whole, as a lowly hourly worker, is a recipe for burnout. This is also probably why I have never advanced into management. Also, it's a dirty capitalist trick.

I was reminded of the time I worked for the Gap briefly when I was twenty years old and desperate for a job. During the training session the manager said to the group of young recruits, "Now remember—when you're wearing this Gap nametag, your actions represent the Gap, so don't forget to take off your nametag before you leave work!" She demonstrated the action, holding up a nametag and a blue polo shirt she'd been using earlier as an example of appropriate work garb.

She smiled and continued. "In fact, one of our employees from last year forgot to take his nametag off and then got into a fight in the Safeway parking lot and was arrested by the police. It made the news and he was described as a 'local Gap employee!'" She looked at the other manager and they both smirked.

I spent my first and only day at the Gap working the dressing rooms. Customers kept asking me how the khakis looked on them. At twenty years old, I found it incredibly awkward to answer them, as it seemed to require commenting honestly on their body parts. Also, business was picking up at the restaurant where I'd worked before and I wanted to get a job there instead.

But when I quit over the phone, newly educated in the evils of capitalism from my brief stint at the Evergreen State College, I felt I had a chance to criticize what I saw as over-the-top consumerism. I told the manager I didn't want to encourage people to buy clothes made in the third world, probably under sweatshop conditions. "And," I mumbled, summoning the courage to condemn the entire industry, "people don't really need to buy that many clothes. I feel like I am encouraging consumerism."

She calmly replied that I wasn't forcing anyone to buy the clothes. "It's their choice if they want to buy the clothes or not," she said. She sounded as if she'd heard it all before, as if she'd used this line on reluctant employees in the past. She did not, however, argue with my assertion that Gap clothing had been made in a sweatshop.

"Well, I can't come in again," I said.

"Thanks for letting me know," she said.

My father, a proud union member, has given me one piece of advice in regard to jobs: "Fuck them before they fuck you." And I suppose on a certain level I have taken it to heart. This sentiment is not to say that I have hated all the bosses and jobs I've ever had. Instead it's a warning: The company will always care more about a nametag than they care about you. It's not personal. Basically, the manager at the Gap was telling me: *It doesn't matter what you do. You could be anyone.*

And so it went with onshore hospitality. The guests pretended to be nice to me, and I pretended to care about the water pressure in their cabin. It's amazing any kind of genuine human interaction happened at all. And yet it did.

The most honest conversation I had with cruise ship guests happened on the last day of the fall tour season. One couple from Singapore, by way of India and Hong Kong, sat and talked with me for nearly an hour. They were fascinating and seemed very intelligent. Their children lived in the United States and in India. He'd owned his own shipping company and had done very well for himself. Theirs was the last flight of the night and they waited with me until nearly six.

As we talked, the man pulled out a shopping bag from Walgreens and emptied it onto the round conference table.

It was all chewing gum, several different brands and flavors. I thought this was odd, but didn't say anything. He opened up a pack and put two pieces of Juicy Fruit into his mouth and began furiously chewing.

"I've never been to India, but I would like to go," I said. "My friend who lives there told me to prepare myself for poverty unlike anything I've seen here." I told them I'd seen a documentary about the slums of Mumbai. "I couldn't believe the living conditions," I confessed. "I mean they were even worse than what, I guess, I had imagined them to be." I described the children sleeping on the floor underneath welding tables and the lack of clean water.

The woman shook her head. "Yes, they are terrible," she said. She had slid down onto the floor and was leaning her head on her large rolling luggage.

The man smiled, and threw his hands up in the air. "But you ask anyone who lives in the slum … they love the slum! They don't want to leave!"

I found this to be a vast oversimplification of the facts but I didn't want to start an argument; these two seemed genuine and we had another hour to kill before they were to leave. "Well, these conditions were really bad …" I said again. Besides, I wanted to say, he was expressing the exact same sentiment as the wealthy Indians in the documentary.

Something changed in the man's face when I wouldn't simply agree with him. He started talking about international banking fraud. "The banks run everything!" he said and dug the giant wad of gum out of his mouth and folded it up in a silver wrapper.

The woman stood up and adjusted the long scarf around her neck. "The United States used to be a great country," she said, not looking directly at me. She fingered some of the gum on the table, and then tossed it aside absentmindedly. "Not anymore. They don't care about their own people anymore." She wandered towards the window, tired of the conversation.

Her husband recommended a couple of books on the subject, as he could tell I was interested. He talked about how crooked the system was, how mortgage rates were fixed by a bank in London. "And it trickles down to everyone." He picked up his cup of Starbucks coffee. "Even down to how much your coffee costs. It affects everybody. And why everyone isn't outraged, I'm not sure!"

"Well, I don't think the average person understands any of that. They just care about how they're going to feed their family."

The man spread his fingers out on the table in between the crumpled bits of gum wrapper. "You know, I think once everyone gets educated on how crooked this system is"— he looked at me—"there's going to be something like the bloody French Revolution."

"I think you're dead right," I nodded. "People are getting sick and tired of the wealth inequality." I don't know what came over me. Talking politics with guests was something I usually tried to avoid. Maybe the fact that they weren't American made me feel more comfortable. But I had to wonder what he meant by referencing the French Revolution. Was he merely saying there would be a revolution, or that it would be incredibly bloody? In this scenario wealthy people like him would be headless in short order.

His wife looked a little uncomfortable.

I turned to her and smiled. "You know, armed revolution isn't exactly polite conversation to be having in the hospitality room."

We all laughed.

But then I couldn't help myself. I turned back to the man. "But you're right," I said. "It's just a matter of time."

The man opened up a different brand of gum, and stuck two more pieces in his mouth. He looked up at me. "We can't get gum in Singapore," he said through a vigorous clench of his jaw. "It's illegal."

"Oh." I remembered Singapore suddenly. The caning incident.

"We have to chew it while we can!" his wife laughed from her spot near the window.

When it was time for them to leave, the man handed me the shopping bag full of gum. "Here," he said. "You can have it, or give it to someone who might need it."

The Two-Hundred-Dollar Roommate

BEFORE YOU CAN HAVE a two-hundred-dollar roommate, you need a two-hundred-dollar room. Look for a house with fifteen-year-old carpets and a dirt basement filled with the belongings of past tenants. The two-hundred-dollar room is an office or a utility room, a basement, a pantry, or a walk-in closet with a carpet thrown down. The two-hundred-dollar room won't have a window or closet or insulation. Of course, the rest of the house isn't insulated either.

You and your housemates are a little desperate, or laissez-faire, or both. You figure the two hundred dollars will help you buy heating oil or a bus pass and some beer. If anything it will enable you to attend more shows. There will be no interview for the two-hundred-dollar roommate. Your standards will be low. He will be the musician friend of your poet friend. He will be the soon-to-be-ex-boyfriend of your soon-to-be-ex-coworker. He will usually be a he.

Things will begin pleasantly enough. But soon you will be disappointed in your two-hundred-dollar roommate. He will use your bar soap. He will eat your food. He will never buy laundry detergent or toilet paper. Every month you will have to extract the rent from him. He will be home all the time using your computer and printing things on your printer and not buying replacement ink cartridges.

He will bring back strange women from the bar. He will invite drug dealers over. You will like all of his friends but you won't like him. Pretty soon you will be talking about him in hushed tones with your other roommates. You'll never know if he is home or not because he doesn't ever leave his room except to steal your food.

On the other hand, sometimes the two-hundred-dollar roommate is your landlord. The two-hundred-dollar roommate has been charging you too much rent, but it doesn't dawn on you until you realize you haven't seen him sober for months. Or sometimes the two-hundred-dollar roommate is the homeowner's ex-girlfriend, who he's still in love with, who falls asleep on the couch in the living room in the afternoon with her mouth open while the TV blares Marx Brothers movies.

The best-case scenario is that the two-hundred-dollar roommate is a medical student or a rock climber who works the graveyard shift in the meat department. The worst-case scenario is that the two-hundred-dollar roommate is your four-hundred-dollar roommate's brother who is going through a mental health crisis and never gets a job or moves out and ends up drawing all over the walls of your bedroom and who you later find out brings home crack addicts that scare the other two-hundred-dollar roommate who is holed up in the laundry room with pneumonia and is avoiding paying rent. In this scenario you lose most of your deposit money.

Sometimes, you will be the two-hundred-dollar roommate. Sometimes your old roommates won't talk to you anymore. Sometimes they are the ones burning bridges. You never burned any bridges. You don't even know why they won't speak to you anymore. Even though it's been over ten years since you've lived with them, you still have dreams about them. In the dreams they are having babies or dying, but they won't touch you or they look the other way when you speak to them.

You live alone now. You have a good thing going.

But sometimes, as you do your dishes in your one-bedroom apartment in the suburbs, you wonder what they're charging for laundry rooms in the city nowadays. Maybe a two-hundred-dollar room now goes for three fifty or even four hundred dollars. Or maybe the people who live in those houses don't want a two-hundred-dollar roommate these days. Maybe they don't need a two-hundred-dollar roommate. Maybe they've turned that laundry room into a craft room. Maybe they're actually using the office as an office or have a treadmill and a litter box in there. Maybe they don't worry about buying heating oil or going to shows.

Outside your window you can hear the traffic merging onto the highway that runs out of town, out to the mountain. It rushes by day and night, never stopping. This apartment is cheap but you don't like the traffic noise, the cars constantly leaving. You've thought about moving back into the city, but it wouldn't be the same. All the people are old and all the buildings are new. No one you know has a two-hundred-dollar roommate anymore. And with your hands in the dishwater, you find yourself crying. You don't know who you're crying for. You're confused. Things are better now, aren't they?

The End of My Career

THE WOMAN SEEMED INTERESTED in the fact that I was a writer; strong people and writing skills were a requirement.

"In fact," she said, "our other claims investigator is a writer, too. She writes romance novels!"

I stared at the water glass and medications sitting on my bedside table as she asked me questions about my résumé. In looking for a new part-time job I had two criteria: The job had to pay at least fifteen dollars an hour, and it had to be flexible. These criteria would help me while I studied to get my real estate license and get into business with my mom as her real estate partner. After a few weeks of searching and applying, this woman called from the HR department of a private investigation firm, which I will refer to as Marley & Marley Investigations. She was calling from the California branch; if I got the job I would be the first claims investigator at their new branch in Portland.

I asked the woman for a basic description of the job. It boiled down to this: When workers' comp insurance companies are unsure about certain claims, they hire Marley & Marley to investigate. Sometimes this entails surveilling the

106

claimant's home and activities to make sure they were truly as injured as they claimed or, in my case, to call the claimants and ask them background questions. "Like if they are filing for bankruptcy or something," the HR woman explained.

"So I need to find out other reasons they might be filing the claim," I said. "I mean, obviously besides the injury itself. What if people lie?"

"Well, we can only ask the claimants the questions and if they lie to us, that's not our problem," she said. "Of course," and here she snickered, "we want to save our clients money." As a claims investigator, she told me, I would need to pay attention to detail. I was good at that. I imagined a scenario in which I discovered that a claimant had previously injured his wrist in a snowboarding accident, and that his house was currently going into foreclosure, and I imagined myself dutifully recording this information. I knew next to nothing about this side of the insurance industry and decided that that fact alone would make the job interesting.

The HR woman, on the other hand, seemed only interested in whether I was able to perform the basic functions of the job: talking to strangers, asking potentially invasive questions, and writing up grammatically correct reports in a timely manner.

I felt a little flattered, actually, that my writing skills would be valued in this new job. I lack discipline and willpower and have never been good at making money from my writing or my zine. If you count actual hours spent writing, this was far and away the most lucrative offer I'd ever gotten in exchange for my writing.

The next day, my father, an electrician in his early sixties, accidentally shot himself in the hand with a nail gun. No actual nail went through his hand—rather, the plunger slammed against his palm after the gun misfired. A small bone in his palm was broken and the doctors told him he needed surgery. This immediately sent my father into a mini-depression. "They're going to take my van away," he said, staring despondently at the TV.

"That sucks, Dad. I'm sorry."

He hit the mute button on the kung fu film he was watching. I knew what the van symbolized: responsibility, respect, hard work. He'd worked for the company for nearly ten years and had "earned" the van. Without it he was just another aging blue-collar worker with an injured hand.

My father shrugged. "I can't blame anybody but myself. It was a stupid accident. There's no excuse."

I felt horrible for him. And also a bit worried. He was the primary breadwinner in our household, which included my mother, a real estate agent who made less than half of what he did, and myself, a chronically ill adult dependent. If my father lost his job altogether, I didn't know how we would make it as a household.

He was put on light duty, which meant that he was stuck in a cubicle doing busy work with his bandaged arm next to another poor sap who'd also injured himself.

One week later, I became the first claims investigator for Marley & Marley in the Pacific Northwest.

"Now you'll have to go down to Salem to take the PI exam," said Josh, the manager of the firm's Portland branch, when he called me after the interview.

"PI? You mean private investigator? Like a private eye?"

"Yeah, but don't worry about it," he said, noting the hesitation in my voice. "It's an open-book test and it really doesn't have anything to do with what you'll be doing, anyway. You'll just be calling claimants up, interviewing them about their claims, and writing up reports. The license is just a formality."

Josh told me that he would take care of scheduling the exam for me. "We'll get you down there, you'll take the test, and you should be up and running in the next few weeks," he said.

But it turned out the next test date in Salem, at the Department of Public Safety Standards and Training, the same institution that trains our cops, wasn't for another month. In the meantime, Josh told me, I could do "ride-alongs" with him to interview some claimants. His main job was surveillance, not taking statements, and he was looking forward to getting those off his plate and onto mine.

Before becoming a licensed PI, I had to get bonded and have my fingerprints and a passport-quality photo taken. I ended up getting this done at a run-down old house on 82nd in Southeast Portland. I could have gotten it done at a police station, but their hours were weird and it was expensive.

It was a muggy June day when I arrived; my hair stuck to my neck and I wiped sweat from my forehead as I parked my car around the corner and walked through a gravel lot to the big yellow house.

As I approached, a woman walked out the front door with a little boy in her arms and a stack of papers in her hand. "Are you going in there?" She pointed with her head to the house.

"Yeah," I said.

"Worst customer service ever!" She walked down the steps, struggling with her squirming son.

"Oh really?" I frowned. I had looked on the internet for places to get my fingerprints taken and this was the cheapest and most convenient location I'd found, but I figured I would indulge this woman since she seemed so upset. Plus given her attitude, it seemed rude to just shrug her off and keep walking.

The woman put her son down next to her car and showed me the papers in her hand. "I just needed to get my fingerprints taken for my nursing job and that *lady* in there was just so *rude* to me."

The woman's son started climbing onto the back of the car, scrambling up the bumper and onto the back window. I asked her what happened.

"There was a dog in there, behind a gate, and I have a very well-behaved child. He just wanted to say hi. That lady *yelled* at him: 'Stay away from the dog!' So rude." While she talked, her son started jumping up and down on the trunk of her car. "He wasn't even doing anything!"

I wondered if she was trying to talk me out of going into the business. "I'm sorry," I said. Her son starting screaming and jumping up and down with his hands in the air. "Worst customer service I've *ever* had," she repeated.

"Well," I said. "Sorry about that ... have a nice day!" And I walked into the house.

Once inside, I saw a grumpy-looking Chow behind a gate in the house's kitchen. A woman glanced up from a large computer screen where it looked like she was gambling. "Fingerprints?" she asked with an air of annoyance.

There was another desk against the corner and the rest of the small front room was filled with Chinese herbs, calendars, and small knickknacks for sale. The woman notarized some papers and took my picture. Another customer walked in while she was taking my fingerprints but she said nothing to him, only motioned with her head toward one of the cheap office chairs against the wall.

The whole thing cost me fifteen dollars and I paid her in cash. The woman wrote me a receipt and walked into another room to retrieve my photo from the printer. She stapled it onto my fingerprint sheet, stuck it into a plastic sleeve, then into a manila envelope, and handed it to me. Without so much as a "good afternoon" she beckoned the waiting man to the fingerprint table.

In my car, I rolled down the window while I waited for the air conditioner to start working. Before driving away, I pulled the fingerprint sheet out of the manila envelope and looked at the photo. Sure enough, the camera had been placed a little below eye level and my weak chin looked nonexistent, plus I wasn't smiling, plus my bangs were plastered to my forehead with sweat, plus the medical alert dog tag I have to wear, ever since my adrenalectomy several years ago, hung down and out of the shot as if I had a booking number around my neck. I looked like a murderer. I looked like Charlize Theron from that movie *Monster*.

I started telling my friends that I was going to be a private investigator and without fail everyone was impressed. I will admit that I thought it was pretty cool, too. At the same time I knew it wasn't going to be a glamorous job. Also, because of all the medical bureaucracy I've had to deal with in my own life, I wondered if I really wanted to be working for insurance companies. But I reminded myself that the job fit all my basic requirements and that it was important to keep an open mind. I hadn't started yet, how did I know what the job would be like?

A week or so later, Josh called, asking me to ride with him the next day to a small town southeast of Portland.

I searched my wardrobe in dismay. It turned out that I'd worn my only presentable shirt to the interview. I couldn't wear that again. Plus it was so tight in the shoulders that it dug into my armpits and made me sweat uncontrollably. And every "nice" dress I owned seemed to show an inappropriate amount of cleavage. I was embarrassed standing there in front of my closet; I had enough outfits to go on thirty internet dates, but nothing to wear for my first day on the job as a private investigator. There was hardly anything wearable that wouldn't be too hot. I settled on a slightly low-cut sleeveless dress.

The next day I met Josh at the Marley & Marley office. There was nothing much to be said about the office except that there was no sign outside the door or any identifying markers. It was in the basement of a large house that had been converted to office space, and the low-ceilinged and windowless rooms smelled overwhelmingly of air freshener. I felt my eyes begin to water.

Josh introduced me to my other coworker, Randy, a grumpy, chubby young man who, I later learned, wore almost exclusively purple polo shirts and brought his pug Sheila to work with him every day. Randy was the head of "operations" and spent most of his day in front of the computer, doing computer stuff, like burning CDs of surveillance footage, emailing things, and putting files together. Randy had been working for Marley & Marley for a few years, but he appeared to hate his job, didn't much like moving here from California, and didn't like the traffic or the rain. At the same time, after only a few minutes of conversation, I could tell that he was the type of person who would probably find something to complain about wherever he went, and that he probably knew this about himself and this is why he stayed. We got into Josh's suv, a fancy one with a computer in the dash, and he plugged in the address to the diner where we were meeting the claimant, a resident aide at a nursing home, who had hurt her back. On the way Josh and I talked about our lives. I told him how I'd just broken up with my boyfriend a few days earlier. It was a guy I met on OkCupid and Josh shared with me that he also used the site, but had had bad luck. He told me about his childhood in the Midwest, how he got into doing PI work in the first place, how he liked Portland and all the live music there is to see in the area. I found out Josh loved his dog, Bart, and that he wanted to hire another office person to assist Randy, and to bring another surveillance guy up from California. "My plan is to retire in fifteen years or so," Josh said, "and spend the rest of my days golfing."

For my part, I told Josh briefly about my Cushing's Disease, why I wore the medical alert tag, all my medications, and how I'd applied for federal disability benefits because I'd been unable to have a full-time job for the last five years or so. I told him I'd worked in food service for ages and couldn't do that kind of work anymore due to my chronic pain. "You're not going to hold that against me, are you?" I joked.

Josh shook his head and rolled his eyes as if I'd just said something ridiculous.

When we arrived at the diner, Josh parked his car at the edge of the parking lot, stating that he always liked to park away from the door. This way he could arrive and leave out of sight of the claimant; if he had to do surveillance later, he wanted to make sure they didn't know what kind of car he was driving.

The claimant was a squirrelly little woman who looked about forty-five. She was thin and her hair was dyed purple. She met us at the diner in what looked to be her teenage daughter's pajamas, and had the air of someone who had at one time been addicted to meth. The waitress sat us at an oversized booth and we all ordered coffee, but no food. This annoyed the waitress, but no one else seemed to notice. Josh got out the interview form, a digital recorder, and a pen. The claimant put her fuzzy leopard-print purse on the table and plopped down her green rabbit's foot keychain on top of the huge laminated menu.

Josh began by reading a short prepared statement at the beginning of the interview. Among others things, he informed her that this conversation was going to be recorded, and asked her for her permission to do so. He also asked if she was under the influence of any drugs or alcohol that may impair her ability to answer the questions. Lastly, he explained that he was a "representative of" the insurance company that had sent us the assignment, and that it was important that she answer the questions truthfully.

The woman answered in the affirmative. As we began the interview, she started to rock back and forth ever so slightly on the brown vinyl diner bench.

The basic interview format is as follows: You ask the claimant personal details about themselves, such as their address, email, phone number. Have they ever been in the armed services or been arrested? Have they had any recent financial difficulties such as bankruptcies, foreclosures, or back taxes? Then you ask about their current position at the job where they injured themselves—how long have they worked there? Who are their managers and coworkers? Would it be okay to contact them regarding the injury? You ask them for a basic description of their job. You ask them to describe how they injured themselves, what they were doing at the time of the injury, if anyone witnessed it. You ask what kind of medical treatment they sought, which doctors they saw, what those doctors said.

Towards the end of the interview you ask them if they have had positive performance reviews and if they have ever had any conflict with coworkers or management. You read another statement at the end, state the time and date of the interview, and turn off the recorder.

That day at the diner, I was surprised by how forthcoming the claimant was; she claimed that other resident aides at the nursing home were out to get her and that she was asked to leave on her last day (she had already put in her two-week notice at the time of the accident and was about to start a new job). She told us that the manager had told her that "it would be better for everyone" if she left. She told us she had no idea what he meant by that. She said that she really needed the workers' comp reimbursement to kick in because she was out of a job now because of her chronic back pain and needed the money. She also claimed that when she told the supervising nurse that she'd injured her back, he'd told her that it was fine and to go back to work. As we ended the interview the woman seemed distracted. She didn't smile, just solemnly shook our hands and walked out of the diner.

Josh and I decided to get lunch somewhere else. We ended up in a quaint little café where we both ordered the clam chowder. Josh told me that most of my interviews would be over the phone, but for more involved cases, like this one with the nursing home, the insurance companies would send us to do in-person interviews. "And that's great," he said.

"Because it means more money for us." He told me I could charge for my travel time and mileage.

After lunch we interviewed the manager in an office at the nursing home. He reported that the claimant in question had been a "problem employee" and that he had asked her to leave on her last day because she was gossiping and "making it a negative work environment." He denied ever having told her that she was fine and to "get back to work." He denied ever having been informed that she was injured at all. "In fact," he said, looking carefully at each of us, "I'm personally offended that anyone would make the claim that I said something like that. I'm a *nurse*. I would never tell someone to go back to work if they were injured."

Throughout the brief interview, the nurse kept looking somewhat nervously at me and then back to Josh. Josh had already explained that I was in training and would only be observing. I'd said next to nothing during both interviews and wondered why, unlike the claimant, the nurse kept staring at me. I wondered if my dress was too revealing. Later, when I got home, I concluded that he was probably staring at me because I was staring at him.

As we left, Josh wondered out loud whether the nurse was lying. I could see no reason why the nurse would lie, but maybe he had been told to lie by the nursing home's administrators. However, the claimant seemed sketchy to me. "Well, you never know. We just take the reports and send them in," Josh sighed, and for the rest of the ride we talked about topics beyond work.

Josh wanted to discuss his experience with OkCupid. In the year that he had been in Portland, he'd had a hard time finding time to date, not to mention finding the right kind of woman. "I want a girl who is spontaneous," he said. "I like to go camping on the weekends. I want to be able to just call a girl on Friday and say, 'Hey, you want to go camping with me tomorrow?' And then we can just fill up my car with some beer and my dog and head to the woods."

I had a hard time imagining doing something like that. I usually have plans every weekend. Dropping them at a moment's notice seemed like a pain in the ass. The last time I dropped everything to go to the beach with a guy was over ten years ago, when I was twenty-three. One summer night, I hopped in my car with this guy from the meat department at the grocery store where I worked. We drove to the beach, paid for a shitty motel room, smoked in bed, and had bad sex. The condom came off inside me and he stopped to ask if I wanted him to "fish it out." I have come to suspect that he also damaged the clutch on my car while driving it. We spent maybe an hour on the beach, ate bad Chinese food, and then got a speeding ticket on the way home. He was three hours late for his shift the next day. He did end up helping me pay for the ticket, but only because, as he told me, his mom told him it was the right thing to do.

"You're looking for a young girl," I told Josh.

He laughed courteously and went on to tell me that he has a hard time trusting women. "I have a lot of female friends. That's never been a problem. It's just being in a relationship, I haven't ever been able to make it work for very long." When I asked him why, he told me that when he was in high school his girlfriend had cheated on him and that everyone found out about it before he did.

"It was humiliating," he said. "Ever since then, I just can't seem to get close to a girl."

He went on to tell me how he'd been on a few dates with a woman recently from OkCupid but that he couldn't tell if she liked him. "I mean, she says she likes me and that she's not seeing other men. But how do I know if that's true?" Josh sighed and looked silently out at the highway. "I don't know, maybe I need therapy," he muttered.

I couldn't imagine how one bad experience in high school could turn a man against women forever. Josh seemed like a pretty nice guy to me. He'd also already told me that he moved to Portland with a girlfriend and that after their seemingly amicable breakup, they'd remained friends and shared custody of his dog.

"You know, that experience sounds awful," I said. "But have you ever thought that maybe the reason you think women are lying to you is that your whole job involves following people around, trying to catch them in a lie?"

"Yeah," he said. "Maybe."

I told Josh about my friend who worked for a women's crisis line and how she had to eventually quit the job because listening to stories of rape and abuse all day made her distrustful of all men and afraid to sleep alone at night. Then I realized that I was trying to talk my boss into quitting his job, so I changed the subject.

As we pulled off the freeway into Portland, I wondered if this was why all private eyes in movies and books are portrayed as cynical and world-weary; they were always dealing with the dark side of humanity.

Josh asked me whether I liked to go see live music.

I couldn't tell if he was asking me out on a date, so I just answered honestly. "I used to go a lot. But not lately. I don't have the time and I'm usually too tired to stay up that late."

My second ride-along was less interesting. The claimant was another nursing home worker who'd injured her back, and it was another in-person interview. But there was nothing controversial about this case. No he said/she said. From what I could tell, there was no reason why the insurance company had sent us out to the middle of nowhere to conduct the interview. When we got back to the office, Josh showed me how to write up the report.

"It's kind of tedious," he said. "But you get the general point."

Since there was nothing I could see that was suspicious about the case, I wondered why the insurance company would spend so much money hiring us to drive two-plus hours to interview this claimant.

"What's the cost–benefit analysis on sending us to interview these people?" I asked Josh. "It just doesn't make sense to me that they would spend so much money for us to make these trips to interview folks."

"A lot of times, these adjusters just don't have the time," Josh answered. "They're swamped with work, and they just want to get it done."

This answer didn't satisfy me; something about Josh's response seemed evasive. I knew this much: Businesses exist to generate profit. I knew what we charged the clients for our services, and I knew what I made as a wage. The insurance companies must have done the math at some point; it couldn't just be about expediency. Then again, what did I know? Maybe the individual adjusters did have control over how certain funds were spent. Maybe they could choose to spend some of that on delegating tasks to PI firms. But no matter how I looked at it, I couldn't shake the feeling that something was fishy.

Josh isn't as smart as me, I thought. That's what it was. He doesn't really understand what's going on here. If he did, why wouldn't he just answer my questions? Was he just naturally incurious?

Finally, the day came for me to go to Salem and take the exam. Josh assured me that I would pass with flying colors, and that everything would be covered beforehand in a class. Plus, he reminded me, it was an open-book test.

The woman leading the class had us all go around and introduce ourselves and explain why we were getting our PI license. Out of the twenty or so people in the room, only one other woman and I weren't ex–law enforcement or claims investigators renewing a pre-existing license. To make matters worse, it turned out that the short class had nothing to do with the test. It was just about who to call if we had problems with the licensing board.

While the teacher talked, we were supposed to fill out a handout. On the first page, next to a cheesy clip art puzzle with the words "Core Values" printed on it, we wrote down *character, honesty, striving for justice, public trust, respect for the laws and constitution of this state and nation.* Then we filled in the names and titles of some administrators on the PI board.

Then we had a twenty-minute break before the exam.

After drinking some coffee and eating an apple and string cheese and spending a few minutes staring at the burned and mangled pieces of the Pentagon from 9/11 displayed in the lobby, I walked back upstairs to take the test.

I was in for another surprise: The "open book" was a five-hundred-page binder of Oregon law material. The proctor passed out the binder and the score sheet. Looking over the questions, I began to feel nervous. So much legal jargon made my eyes cross. Also, even though the answers were all in the book, would I be able to find them? To answer the first question, I needed to find the legal definition of harassment. I found myself flipping endlessly through the book. Multiply that by two hundred questions and you get an idea of the tedium of the test.

An hour later, when I was finished, I looked up and realized that everyone else was still reading and searching away. But hey, I was smart, right? I had a master's degree, right? But I didn't want to be the first person done with the exam. I decided to wait until someone got up first. Eventually, the other woman in the class, who, of course, was also taking the test cold, stood up and handed in her answer sheet. And then I did the same.

A couple of days later I got an email from DPSST; I had failed the test by one question. I burst into tears. What was I going to tell Josh? I knew how frustrated he was that we had already had to wait so long for me to take the test in the first place, and how eager he was to get the statements off his plate so he could focus on growing the business. To top it off, he was going to think I was an idiot. Who fails an open-book test? I'd always been a good student and I hated having to admit failure.

I called my new boyfriend Bernard and told him I'd failed the test. I was so disappointed, but by the end of the conversation he had me laughing about it. So I took a deep breath, summoned up the courage to call Josh, and left a message on his voicemail. "Look, Josh," I said. "I failed the PI exam. I understand if you want to hire a new claims investigator. I'm very embarrassed and disappointed."

He called me back twenty minutes later.

"I got your message," he said, his voice kind, but tired-sounding. He sighed. "Look, don't worry about it. I don't want to go through the whole hiring process again. We'll just get you scheduled again and do it as soon as we can."

I went about getting the exam rescheduled for two weeks later.

Then, two days later, I found out that I'd also failed the fingerprint test. DPSST told me that my prints were of unacceptably low quality. I was going to have to get them done again. I called the place on 82nd where I'd gotten them taken and told the woman that I needed to get my fingerprints re-done and asked if she would do it for free.

"Yes, but only one more time. After that you can go somewhere else."

"Do you know why they would reject them like this?" I asked her out of curiosity.

"All you nurses wash your hands too much and wash your fingerprints off, and then we can't get a good print off of you!" she shouted into the phone.

A notice came in the mail that my hearing before a disability judge would finally take place in early June. Strangely, even though I had longed for the chance to plead my case before a judge, I was afraid.

A couple of years ago I applied for federal disability; I had finally accepted that I could not continue working in food service anymore because of my Cushing's Disease (an overabundance of cortisol), and the realization that I might never be able to have a normal life was starting to dawn on me. I would get weak after only a few hours of work. If I didn't get a good night's rest my whole body hurt. Now I had Addison's Disease (a deficit of cortisol) and I was diagnosed with fibromyalgia and hypopituitarism. I didn't want to see myself as disabled and I certainly didn't want to consign myself to a life of poverty. Nevertheless, when my case was denied, I refused to give up, and filled out the necessary documentation and got a lawyer.

There's this thing that happens when you're sick: People don't believe you. I can't tell you how many times I have faced disbelief, dismissal, and downright contempt from people who don't want to believe that the seemingly healthy person in front of them is actually incapable of holding down a full-time job.

I have myself been one of these doubters. There was a man who I used to work with at the grocery store in Southeast Portland. His name was James. James was a rail-thin hip hop fan from Wisconsin who had moved to Portland with his dreadlocked fiancée, a pale vegetarian who worked in the meat department of the same store. James had a back injury from a previous job and after six months of moving twenty-five to thirty-pound bowls of potato salad in and out of the deli case, he was in so much pain he could barely stand. He was eventually put on light duty, which annoyed the other workers; without the ability to lift or stand for long periods of time, he was useless as a deli worker. I remember sneering, "Why doesn't he just get another job?"

James did end up leaving his job at the deli. Through the rumor mill, I remember hearing that he was filing for workers' comp through the store's insurance even though his injury had supposedly been sustained at another job. The person who reported this to me showed no compassion for James. I don't remember what my reaction was, and I don't remember hearing anything more about James.

Years later, when I got sick with Cushing's Disease and had to use a stool to do my job, when I was often able to go home early or do work at a desk instead of at the cheese counter, I thought of James. His thin face floated into my consciousness like some ghost of delis past and demanded, "*Now* who should get another job?"

Over the years I have downplayed my illness, making

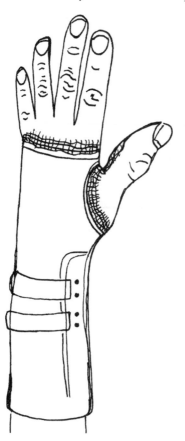

light of it, cracking jokes at my own expense, and generally trying to pretend that I am not as sick as I really am. I found myself dropping the hearing notice in a pile of unsorted receipts and trying to forget about it.

But as my court date approached, I had to ask myself why I hadn't called my lawyer. Wasn't this what I wanted? Wouldn't getting the disability status be totally redemptive? I began to realize that the reason I didn't want to appear before a judge was because going before the judge meant I had to tell my story, and telling my story is exhausting; being met with skepticism is crushing. This is why people don't report rape or other violent crimes, why witnesses refuse to testify, why adult children of abuse let their abusers walk free. Telling your story becomes more painful the more you are questioned and doubted. Often your story makes no sense to you, yourself. You have to wonder if you're just dramatizing or being hysterical. You find yourself asking: *Did this really happen to me?* It doesn't fit within the narrative of what I always thought my life was supposed to look like.

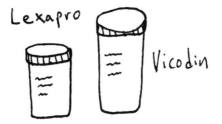

Telling my story, really telling it, often feels like I'm enacting a masochistic theater of victimization. If I tell the judge how bad it's really been for me, then I have to tell myself. Parading my suffering in front of a judge, who would, well, judge me, sounded like the worst thing ever. I certainly didn't want to hear my story again.

I thought about it. I lost sleep over it. I cried about it with friends and my mother. Ultimately, I decided that if I relinquished my right to a hearing I would regret it the rest of my life. It was time to be brave.

The tricky thing was that I had actually begun to feel better. In January, after almost collapsing at an Indian restaurant in Southeast Portland, I'd realized that my total daily medication dose, of the steroids I need to live, was too low. So I had upped my dose of steroids and noticed marked improvements. I still hadn't taken on full-time work, and I still doubted that I ever could, but it felt wrong to give up on the chance to make a middle class wage as a realtor … if, in fact, I was able to do it.

I came up with a plan: I was going to apply for back pay for my disability. This meant I would forgo an ongoing monthly payment and instead make the argument that for a period of time I had been disabled, and therefore deserved back pay, or a lump sum.

A week later, I walked into my lawyer's Lake Oswego office and took a seat in the small waiting room. It was a shabby kind of place and looked shabbier than I remembered from my appointment last year. Obviously there wasn't much money in helping disabled people.

My lawyer was a kind older man with dark hair and glasses, full of empathy and consideration. He thanked me for coming in and gestured to the chair opposite his desk. He took notes as we went over my medical history again. I was relieved to hear that he supported my plan to file for back pay. He told me that if I thought I might be able to take on work, even if it were part time, it was better than "sitting around the house getting depressed." He thought I had a good case and told me it looked impressive that I had worked a bit over the last few years. "The judges like to see that people are making an effort," he said.

After we were done with my medical history and the particulars of what we would say to the judge, he leaned back in his chair. "So what are you doing for work these days?" he asked.

I'd honestly been hoping he wouldn't ask. "Well," I said, "I've been cleaning houses, mostly. But I can't do it that much because it's too hard on my body, so I recently got a part-time job as a claims investigator. You know, for workers' comp claims."

A dark cloud passed over my lawyer's face. He said nothing.

"I don't really know what it's going to be like," I stammered. "I'm just starting out. I just hope it doesn't turn out to be shitty working for insurance companies."

"That's a horrible industry," my lawyer said, shaking his head. "Do you know what they do to people? Those 'doctors' they hire to evaluate people's medical conditions ... they purposefully put their offices on the second story and, you know, there will be no elevators. So people have to climb the stairs. Then, the insurances companies use this as evidence against them later. They say, 'Well, you were well enough to climb the stairs!' Even though the people were required to go to these doctors and didn't think they had any choice but to climb the stairs!"

I grimaced. "Well, yeah," I said. "I know." Although I didn't know.

"Um," I went on, "I think that I'm going to wait and see, though. I mean, I haven't really started yet, plus it doesn't involve any physical work and I can use my writing skills. I needed something flexible to work around my health issues." As I tried to explain myself, my lawyer just got this very sad look on his face and changed the subject. He thanked me for my time and told me he would see me a week later at my hearing. I left his office feeling as if I'd just disappointed my grandpa.

Before my second test, Bernard cooked me eggs and sausage for breakfast and gave me the pep talk of a lifetime. And yet I was nervous all morning, suffering through several bouts of diarrhea by the time I got into my little Honda and headed back down to Salem. But at least Bernard's words stuck with me, and besides, with one go-round under my belt, I knew that all I had to do was systematically look up every term until I found the exact right answer in the book. No more relying on my generally astute intuition.

When I pulled into the parking lot there were about fifteen cops running and doing jumping jacks in the blistering heat. I walked by them, feeling a little cagey, as is usual for me around law enforcement.

I took the test alone in a small, windowless room on the first floor behind the front desk.

This time I only had to wait half an hour for my results. The woman at the front desk smiled as she approached the glass separating the reception desk from the lobby. "Congratulations," she said. "You passed the test!"

"What a relief!" I said. "How many questions did I miss?" I asked out of curiosity.

"You only missed two."

"Which ones?"

The woman frowned. "I'm sorry," she said, "I'm not permitted to say."

I nodded. That made sense—they didn't want me passing on any information to future test-takers. I took the license and slid my cell phone through the window. "Hey, do you mind taking my picture?"

She laughed. "No problem!" While I held my certificate next to my face, she took several photos of me.

I posted the photo on Facebook and Instagram. By the end of the day, 160 people would like the photo and thirty people would go so far as to congratulate me.

"Thanks so much!" I said to her and walked outside to call Josh and text Bernard.

The cops were still jogging in the summer heat as I pulled

out of the parking lot and headed for the highway. Soon I approached the Santiam Correctional Institution. The exercise yard faces the highway and I could see fifty or so shirtless inmates jogging around the track. As I swept past, as if on cue, they all slowed momentarily, heads turning in unison, and looked at my long blond hair flapping out the open window.

A few days later I took the elevator to the fourth floor of the federal building and hurried down the hallway to the disability waiting room. I was in such a rush that I almost walked right by the cop who was sitting at a desk by the door. He patted me down and asked to see my ID. These small rituals made me feel even more anxious about what lay ahead. Like the DMV and post office, the room smelled funky and dusty. My lawyer was waiting for me with a restless look on his face; due to unexpected traffic, I was twenty minutes late.

I apologized for being late and we were ushered into the courtroom. I sat at one end of a long table with my lawyer, each of us in front of a microphone. There was a young male court reporter in the room as well as the judge, an older white man. The judge joked with me a bit before the proceedings started. It turned out he used to shop at the grocery store where I'd sold cheese. "I live right up the street!" he said and smiled. Then he swore me in and started asking me questions. I was surprised because I did most of the talking. I hadn't expected this. I'd thought my lawyer would do most of the talking.

The judge asked me about my disease, my surgeries, my limitations, and what kind of work I was doing now. I hadn't officially started the PI job yet, so I only mentioned the housecleaning and that I didn't have the energy to clean more than about three houses a week, and no more than one a day. As we talked about my health, I was surprised by how little the judge knew, not only about Cushing's Disease, but the endocrine system in general. I had to explain to him what cortisol is, where the pituitary is located, and all about Addison's Disease. Of course he was not a doctor, he was a judge, but this seemed weird to me, that he would have the power to rule on disabilities while apparently having such little knowledge of the human body. I suddenly felt grateful for the years I'd spent talking and writing about my illness. And for perhaps the first time ever, I felt thankful for the two years I'd spent in grad school studying writing. I thought: *I may not be able to work full time, and I may be in a ton of debt, but at least I can express myself clearly in front of a disability judge who doesn't know where the pituitary is or what it does.*

The judge asked me to explain what happened after my surgery to get my adrenals removed, the surgery that "cured" me of Cushing's, but gave me Addison's. I shared with him what I regard to be the most painful part of my story: After the doctors tried to save my life by operating on my pituitary, that very surgery made my pituitary start shutting down. "Now I have to take all the hormones. Everything except testosterone." My voice started to falter and I found myself crying. I looked down and as if by magic, a box of tissue appeared in front of me. I hadn't noticed it before. I plucked out a few of them and blew my nose.

The judge looked at me with what seemed like empathy. "You're thirty-four?" he said. "And I suppose you are unable to have children now?"

I shrugged my shoulders. "I will probably need help," I said, "but I haven't investigated it." I blew my nose again. The question seemed odd; I didn't understand how my ability to have children was relevant to my disability case. There are plenty of infertile people out there capable of holding down full-time jobs.

The judge frowned sympathetically and let out a sigh. "Thank you for your testimony, Ms. Grover," he said. He then turned and talked to the speakerphone on his desk. It was the female "employment specialist" who had been listening in on a phone line throughout the interview. They talked some gibberish about different numbers, levels of disability, and pay rates. The judge looked down at the stack of papers in front of him and started flipping through them. "Well," he said, "I will probably rule in your favor." He looked up briefly at my lawyer. "Things are a bit backed up now but you should have my ruling in a few months."

And then the trial was over.

I'd learned since becoming ill not to get my hopes up, and so I had no emotional reaction to this news. My lawyer, on the other hand, seemed very excited. He ushered me into a side room. "You did a great job!" he said. "Things are looking good for your case. I can't imagine why the judge would have said that if he wasn't going to give you the full amount."

"That's great!" I said. And yet, I was disconcerted by the whole process. It wasn't what I expected. The decision seemed to rest almost solely on my ability to plead my case. And the question about my fertility weighed on me. What did that have to do with anything? The whole process seemed very arbitrary. I left the building and got into my car, which wouldn't start. It was out of gas.

On Monday, Josh put me right to work, handing over four or five cases. There was a lot to learn. The drill about calling claimants was that you had to keep track of each time you

called them and which number you used. Marley & Marley
used a separate data-gathering service to track down possible
phone numbers and addresses for claimants. It was my responsibility to try every plausible number on the report and
write down all the pertinent details. And there were a lot of
details: claim numbers, employers, dates, injuries.

Plus there was a constant barrage of emails from the
claims adjusters. The adjusters often wanted to know specific
details: For example, was it possible the claimant had injured
himself while hiking? After all, he'd told his managers he
liked to hike. Why had it taken so long for him to file the
claim?

The adjusters filled me in on all sorts of irrelevant details,
often sending me single-line emails stating that the claimant
had been arrested for domestic abuse or had a DUI on his or
her record. This made me uncomfortable, as if the adjusters
were trying to get me to come to negative conclusions about
the claimants before I'd even interviewed them. A standard
question on my interview form was about arrests and in-
carcerations. I wondered what that had to do with whether a claimant had been injured on the job. In the minds of
the adjusters, I supposed, a criminal record made a claimant more likely to commit fraud. I didn't know if I agreed.
Other emails were more vaguely accusatory. *This claimant is
avoiding me,* the adjuster would write. *Tell her if she does not
comply, we'll serve her with a mandatory compliance order.* Or:
This claimant is a real piece of work. Ask her what her BMI is.

I started taking extra doses of my steroids to cope with
the stress. The diarrhea didn't let up.

Yes, I had a PI license, and yes, I was a proxy for the insurance companies. But in reality, I was just a message on
someone's voicemail. They didn't know me and often didn't

know the name of their workers' comp insurance company or TPA (third-party administrator, a supposedly unbiased entity that denies or approves claims). And to make matters worse, I was calling from my personal cell phone. I wasn't a claims adjuster, I was a hired snooper, and my call to a claimant indicated that they were now under investigation, a fact Josh encouraged me to avoid mentioning above all else. I was under strict orders to introduce myself as a representative of the insurance company or a TPA, which was not a lie, but not exactly the whole truth, either.

I learned this the hard way when I finally heard back from one of the claimants. I'd already left a few messages on his voicemail asking him if he could call me back so I could make an appointment to interview him about his claim. He had injured his foot while working at a restaurant in the town where he lived in Washington.

"Now, who are you?" he asked. "How do I know that you're not just some random person trying to get my personal information? You're calling from an Oregon area code. Is this your cell phone?"

He'd caught me off guard; I'd answered my phone while visiting my sister at her house. I walked inside quickly, away from the brunch we were having on her picnic table. "I'm a representative of your employer's insurance company," I said into the phone, realizing immediately that this sounded sketchy, what with my siblings' laughter and traffic noise in the background.

"Yeah, but how do I know that? *Who* do you work for?"

I felt my stomach turn over. Ten seconds into my first professional interview and the jig was already up. I walked upstairs, into my sister's bedroom, and shut the door behind me. "I work for a company called Marley & Marley," I said.

I knew it wasn't kosher to reveal the name of my employer, but I made sure to leave out the "Investigations" part of the title. This immediately felt deceptive.

"My only job is to do this interview," I explained. "I know nothing about your claim, you, or your injury. My only function is just to take this interview, write a report, and send it to your claims adjuster." This was true. This was all true. I was, after all, just a cog in a machine. An impartial, unbiased cog.

There was a long pause on the other end of the line. I stared at the white quilt on my sister's bed while I waited for the claimant to say something. I was a rudderless, morally bankrupt robot and this guy could see right through me.

"Everything inside of me is telling me that it's a really bad idea to talk to you," the man said. And yet I could hear the hesitation in his voice, a hesitation that told me that he just needed a little more assurance from me and he would change his mind. I'd learned this from selling cheese. Sometimes people just need you to tell them that the cheese is, in fact, delicious.

"Look," I went on. "You don't have to do this interview. You don't have to answer any questions you feel uncomfortable with. If it would make you feel more comfortable, I can have my boss, Josh, call you."

The man sighed. "Okay. No, that's fine. Let's just get this over with."

"Right now? Can we schedule a time to do the interview? It takes about an hour." I was in the middle of brunch, after all—I didn't want to drop everything.

"Look, we either do it now or we don't do it. How's that?"

"Okay," I said. "Let me just get my computer out and pull up your files."

"Where are you? You're not at your office?"

"I don't have an office," I stuttered. "I'm a part-time employee. I have to do these interviews wherever I happen to be."

The man grumbled as I struggled to get his file pulled up on my work computer and set up the digital recorder.

Finally I began the interview.

The man was forty-nine years old and lived in a small town that I'd never heard of. He declined to give me his email, home address, or social security number. He told me he had no hobbies. He told me he was single and lived alone. He told me he had an eighth-grade education. He told me that he was wrongfully fired by his ex-employer at the restaurant and that this had been decided by some Washington State governmental body I'd never heard of. "It's a fact," he said. He was annoyed that I had to ask him to explain this further. He was annoyed and impatient at nearly all of my questions and kept asking me why I needed to know. I explained that I was just following a form, that I was just asking, and he was welcome to not answer. I asked him if he used drugs or alcohol and he told me that he used to, but not anymore. I asked him to give me a basic description of his job.

"I'm a pantry chef. You don't know what that means? These are stupid questions."

I asked the claimant who his supervisor was, and how long this person had been his supervisor.

"What? That question makes no sense. How do I know how long he's been the manager?"

"How long has he been *your* supervisor?" I asked again.

"*I don't know.* Since I started working there? This is so stupid. I'm sorry but I really hate stupid questions."

"Okay," I said. I asked him to describe how he injured himself.

"I was breaking down boxes and I hurt my foot."

"And how did that happen?"

"*Weeellll*," he said as if he were talking to a child, "I was going into the garbage area and I was breaking down boxes … do you know what that means?"

"Yes."

"And I kicked one of the boxes with my foot and I felt something snap."

"Did anyone witness your injury?"

"I don't know."

"Did you tell anyone about your injury?"

"No! It's a kitchen. I work ten-, twelve-hour days. You work when there is work to do, and when there's no more work to do you go home. Have you ever worked in a restaurant?"

"Yes, actually I have," I said. "Okay. So you didn't tell anyone?"

"No," the man sighed.

I asked the man if he had ever been arrested.

"That's a matter of public record."

"Have you ever been incarcerated?"

"Like I said, that's a matter of public record."

I asked him where he was currently working. "I'm working at Sandy's."

"What's that?"

"It's a convenience store. Like a 7-Eleven."

"How long have you been working there?"

"Well, Rachel was nice enough to give me my old job back after I got fired from the restaurant. I used to work at Sandy's and that's what makes this whole thing so horrible.

I thought I was going to have a job there, at the restaurant, you know, for the rest of my life."

I felt my stomach drop again. Here was a man with a criminal record and an eighth-grade education and he was working at a convenience store; what kind of future could he possibly have now?

"That sucks," I said. "I'm sorry."

"Yeah."

After the interview I called Josh to talk about how it went. I paced back and forth in my sister's now-empty backyard. "Hey," I said, "I just wanted to check in with you. This guy was really suspicious and did not want to answer my questions."

"Yeah, some people just like being hostile and argumentative. They just want to give you a hard time. You're gonna run into that."

I thought briefly that if I were this guy, who'd obviously had a very hard time, I wouldn't have wanted to talk to me either. I would have been suspicious of my intentions, I would have wondered if the person on the other end of the line was just trying to screw me over like everyone else in my life.

I told Josh what I'd told the claimant, that he was free to not answer questions he was uncomfortable with.

"That's fine. That's a good idea, just don't use the word 'investigation.'"

"Okay," I said. I felt sick to my stomach. I hung up the phone, went into my sister's bathroom, and had diarrhea.

As the week wore on, the diarrhea continued. Also, my hands started hurting from typing up reports. I was familiar with this achy, tight feeling in my hands and forearms—the tendency for them to tingle and fall asleep at night. Before I was diagnosed with Cushing's Disease, while cutting and wrapping cheese at the grocery store, I experienced tingling and pain in my hands, similar to having carpal tunnel syndrome. I'd visited the doctor about it then and he'd told me just to rest my hands if I could and to stop doing artwork outside of work for a while. He also suggested that I get arm braces, just in case. From time to time when I was typing or drawing a lot, the hand and arm pain would flare up, but for the past few years I'd generally kept it under control. But with this new Marley & Marley job, it had gotten pretty bad pretty quickly. I started wearing my arm braces again, and ordered an ergonomic keyboard because Josh told me the firm would pay for it.

One morning I strapped on my braces and sat down in my quiet living room to record an interview. The claimant worked for a healthcare company in the billing office. She reported that she worked sometimes fourteen hours a day typing and that she had been recently diagnosed with carpal tunnel syndrome and would need surgery on her right hand. Following the claims adjuster's instructions, I asked her many times and in many different ways if she had ever experienced these types of symptoms before. She denied ever having experienced these symptoms in the past. I asked her if she had any extracurricular activities or hobbies. She told me she gardened and watched movies. I couldn't help but wonder how bad my own pain would get if I continued being a private investigator. If I filed a claim against Marley & Marley, another private investigator wouldn't have to look very hard to find the page on my website titled "Martha Grover's Artwork."

That afternoon I went back to the office to write up the report. By this point I had become fairly proficient and could write up the reports while sitting in the main office, with other things going on in the background.

Josh was sitting at his desk making phone calls.

"Hello," he said, "this is Package Delivery Services. We've been having a hard time delivering to your address. The package keeps getting sent back to our warehouse. Will you be home tomorrow between the hours of 10:00 a.m. and 1:00 p.m.?" He paused. "You will? Okay, thanks. That's very helpful."

Next, Josh rang up the surveillance crew. "The claimant will be home tomorrow at 10:00 a.m.," he told them, then leaned forward dramatically in his office chair as he hung up the phone. Josh grinned in my general direction. "And that's how you get it done!"

"Package Delivery Services?" I said, turning to him. "They bought that?"

"You'd be surprised how much information people will reveal to a total stranger. I needed to know when he was going to be home and now I know."

I wanted to say how surprised I was that someone was so stupid, but it seemed insulting to Josh since he seemed to think he was being clever. If someone called me from "Package Delivery Services" I'd immediately be suspicious. But then again, Josh had lied about who he was, so I wasn't actually sure if anyone in this scenario was stupid, exactly.

Josh went on to tell me that people will claim a work-related injury and then post pictures of themselves on Facebook going to Disneyland with their kids.

"That's pretty outrageous," I said. Although I didn't mean *outrageous* necessarily, only perhaps naive. The average person has no idea that by merely filing a workers' comp claim, they set into motion a whole apparatus of loss prevention by the insurance company. Lying about your injury is stupid. Not suspecting that the insurance industry is going to follow your every move? That's actually a normal reaction.

"I saw that we charge clients for social media investigations," I said. "My question is: If people make their posts private, how much information can we get off their Facebook pages?"

"Well, people post stuff on other people's feeds that aren't private," he explained. "And the investigators who do that kind of work have their ways."

I couldn't tell if Josh didn't know the answer to my question or if he was just being evasive. But then, I'd just seen him lie to someone over the phone; it couldn't be that he didn't want to tell me about shady things investigators were doing. I concluded that he didn't actually know and that's why he wasn't answering my question.

I turned back to my report and stared numbly at the page. On one of our ride-alongs, I'd asked Josh if people ever got suspicious about cars being parked in their neighborhood for hours on end.

"All the time," he'd answered. "Sometimes people call the cops, but when they come and knock on your window, you just tell the officer that you are an investigator. The cops will end up telling the neighbors that you're just an out-of-town guest of someone else on the street and that your car will be gone in a few days. If I know I'm going to be surveilling someone for a long time, I call the police ahead of time. That way if someone calls, they can say, 'Oh, someone already called it in.'"

"So the cops will cover for you?" I said. I didn't use the word lie.

"Yes," he said.

On the way home that day I thought about the lie Josh had told the claimant earlier. I thought about how cops are apparently routinely lying to people about what they believe to be suspicious vehicles in their neighborhood. I didn't know if I wanted to do this job anymore. But I didn't want to quit. I seemed to be operating in a morally gray area.

As I continued south, I considered my early childhood as a fundamentalist Christian. In that world, morality is very black and white. As I've matured, stopped identifying as a Christian, and done some soul-searching, I've recognized that black-and-white thinking has influenced me negatively in a lot of ways—number one being that generally the world is just a whole lot more complicated than either/or. I nodded my head. The fundamentalism was at fault. That's why I was having so many doubts about this job. It was time for me to grow up and learn how to function in the morally ambiguous universe of adulthood. I filed the doubts neatly away in a corner of my brain labeled "resolved."

But the diarrhea wouldn't stop. It was full-on summer and I wanted to enjoy it, but I felt awful. I complained to my family on our private Facebook page about the diarrhea and the stress. I didn't post the sentiment on my general feed, because I had become slightly paranoid about mentioning my job online. One of my sisters reminded me that all new jobs are stressful and that I should stick it out, while others expressed sympathy; nobody, including Bernard, told me to quit. They must have recognized how important this job was to me. I had been sick and underemployed for so long, and they were just happy to see me doing something. The job wasn't cleaning houses, which they knew was hard on my body, and it utilized my writing skills. They wanted to see me succeed, to challenge myself, to move out of my parents' house, where I had been living for the last two years.

This job was already heavy with meaning. If I quit, it would mean that I was incapable of supporting myself, that I was a loser. Being thirty-four and still living with my parents had taken a toll on my self-esteem. At the same time, I hadn't told them about my deepest concerns about the ethics of my PI work. Probably because I was afraid that if I did tell them what I was doing (or what I suspected I was doing) they would be horrified and tell me to quit. I didn't want them to tell me to quit—I wanted them to tell me that they wouldn't think I was weak if I did quit. I didn't want them to tell me what to do; I wanted their blessing regardless of what I chose.

I also didn't want to quit because I saw how hard my father worked to help support us. He was doing better, physically anyway; his hand had healed and he was doing regular work again. However, it was without his van—he was now just another worker. His job as a supervisor was taken away. The first couple of days back on the job, when it was clear that he wouldn't get his van back, he looked sad and defeated. He mentioned the van several times. But my father doesn't like to dwell on the negative aspects of his job. "I can't complain," he said. My mother reminded him that the company had always been good to him.

I settled into a routine of phone calls and interviews. I spent about half my time at the office and got to know Monica, Randy's new assistant. She told me that she used to work at a coffee shop and that she enjoyed not having to work in customer service anymore. She seemed like a nice enough person. She was a round, friendly blonde. Like me.

And I reminded myself that I did enjoy some parts of the work; it was good for my writing skills and my schedule was flexible. But this also meant that I could receive a phone call from a claimant at any moment. I have always had a hard time with phone interruptions and so I found myself operating at a low level of anxiety all the time, never knowing when I would have to pull off the road to take a phone call from a confused and often hostile claimant.

Many of the claimants were nursing home workers. But they weren't CNAs (certified nursing assistants), they were resident aides. Which means they did a lot of the physical labor involved in getting very old and often obese residents out of bed, to the toilet, and to their meals in the dining halls. It also meant they earned minimum wage or just a little above it. And the resident aides almost always had back injuries. Often, as with most of the claimants who had bodily injuries, the moment of injury was so very insignificant that it seemed to take on poetic, almost symbolic overtones.

I was bending down to pick up a saucer that fell on the floor, and I heard a snap.

I was getting a box of frozen hash browns off the walk-in shelf.

Buddy let the walk-in door close on my shoulder.

I bent down to pick up a fork, and I heard a snap.

I was trapped under a four-hundred-pound resident, pinned against a bathroom wall for forty-five minutes. It took four other resident aides and a nurse to free me.

I kept asking the management to get us earplugs. I heard a buzzing. I don't shoot guns. I don't lift weights. My only hobbies are watching TV.

I felt a twinge.

I felt a sharp pain.

I was filling the med-trays, over and over.

It started gradually. I didn't notice at first.

I didn't file a claim right away because I thought it would go away.

I felt something snap.

I don't have any hobbies. On the weekends I relax. I hang out with my grandchildren. I got a divorce ten years ago.

The doctor won't keep treating me until I get this claim filled.

I haven't filed for bankruptcy.

The management hasn't been giving me any hours. I think they are going to fire me.

I have never experienced these symptoms before.

I am a hard worker.

I never call in sick.

I show up to work on time.

I was bending over to answer the phone, and something just snapped.

One week Josh asked me to do a "drive-by" of a claimant's house while I was down in her southern Oregon town for a scheduled interview with her. "If we know some information before we send down a surveillance team," Josh told me, "we'll be ahead of the game." He showed me how to position my digital recorder out of sight, by my side in the car seat, and what to say. He wanted a general description of the residence and the license plates of any vehicle parked nearby. Bernard decided to ride with me that day; it was a scenic drive and we thought we might go hiking afterwards.

The drive-by was a near total disaster. This is how I explained it to Monica and Randy back in the operations office. "My boyfriend was driving," I said, grinning. "I told him to park in front of the house, but there were no available parking spots, so he slowed to a stop in the middle of the street. And here I am trying to talk into the recorder and we are stopped in the middle of the street, totally conspicuous! So I tell him to keep driving. So he does and then makes a slow U-turn in the middle of the street. We come back and he doesn't understand what I want him to do, so he makes another U-turn! It was so clumsy, the whole thing. I mean, I did get some plate numbers. But then I realized that the batteries had died on the recorder!" I laughed.

At the time, I thought they might think the story was funny—you know, PIs sharing their foibles over the water cooler. But Monica and Randy just stared at me and said nothing.

"Well," I felt my face turn red. "I guess that's why I should leave surveillance to the pros!" I turned abruptly and walked back to my desk. As I walked away, I heard Randy mutter something. Monica giggled. I felt my stomach turn over. I had become that person in the office. This annoyed me.

I was put on a stress case involving a public employee in a small eastern Oregon town. This was my second public employee stress case. Her lawyer was on a third line and the woman was not only hard to hear, but periodically broke down in tears as I went through the standard questions. The story was long and involved. Her lawyer kept stopping the interview to make sure I understood the basics of what she was telling me, often treating me as if I were a total moron. The claims adjuster had already sent me emails informing me that this woman had filed claims and had sued her employer in the past. The claims adjuster wrote that she "was not surprised" the claimant had hired the same law firm as last time to represent her. I wasn't able to figure out why her choice in lawyer was relevant, other than to insinuate that the claimant was somehow overly litigious. Or greedy, or lazy, or weak.

I mentioned this case to Monica as we momentarily gathered around the microwave in the office supply closet. "How's it going?" she asked.

"These stress cases are stressing me out," I joked. I told her about the woman sobbing on the phone. She was an older woman, close to retirement at the public office where she had spent most of her working life. To me, she had seemed utterly terrified of losing her retirement plan. "I realize that all these older public employees get so routinized, so comfortable in their jobs, that they can't handle change. They get a new manager and they can't handle it."

Monica only giggled nervously and exited the supply closet. *Monica is a moron*, I thought.

I got a new stress case about a week later. The claims adjuster wanted me to interview the claimant's boss and coworker. Their phone numbers provided by our information service, however, were incorrect or discontinued. I asked Josh what I should do. He told me to call the claimant's place of employment and ask them for the numbers. And so I did.

"Well," the receptionist told me, "I know that Mr. Brown [the claimant] isn't filing a stress claim against his current boss. His current boss has only been in the director's position for about a month. I can give you the home phone number of our previous director. That is who you probably want to interview."

I nodded and jotted down both numbers. I felt uncertain about how to proceed; Josh was out of the office and I didn't want to bother him while he was on vacation, so I called up the Marley & Marley office and talked to Randy. I explained to him that the claims adjuster wanted me to interview the claimant's current boss even though the previous boss was the one who had been the claimant's supervisor for the majority of the period of injury. Randy was gruff with me on the phone. "I don't know," he sighed. "All I know is what they send me. It doesn't make any sense to me either."

I also mentioned that there was some confusion regarding the dates of the injury. Between the workers' comp form that the claimant had filled out and the dates on what the claims adjuster had sent to Marley & Marley, it was unclear what period the claimant was referring to. Again, Randy had no answers. He told me to email the claims adjuster. So I did. I asked her about the dates and why she wanted me to interview the current boss, rather than the "problem boss." She didn't reply.

After a twenty-minute bout of diarrhea, I left the house to go babysit my two-year-old nephew, Javi. I picked him up and took him to the park, where, with a vague feeling of unrest in my stomach, I watched him jump up and down at the end of the metal slide. I felt dehydrated and slightly dizzy. My head hurt. I couldn't stop thinking about the stress case. I felt as if I were being asked to do my job poorly. With a man's livelihood and a large medical payout at stake, it seemed like this case was being handled very haphazardly. Why were the dates messed up? Why did they want me to interview the current boss and not the old boss?

I called out to Javi and we sat down on the grass. I pulled out snacks, some sticks of string cheese and nuts. Javi was running around in the grass with a stick of cheese clutched in his hand when my cell phone rang. It was Josh, who was apparently taking a break from his vacation. "Hi Martha," he said. "I'm calling because Cindy, the claims adjuster from the Brown stress case, called me and was concerned about an email you sent her."

I felt a sharp pain in my stomach and sucked in air. I kicked the dirt with my tennis shoe. "She called you? Why?"

"She seemed to be concerned that you didn't know what you were talking about. In the future, just call me first if you have any questions."

"Well, I called Randy and he told me to ask the claims adjuster to clarify some things for me. So that's what I did. The dates don't match up and I'm not sure why she would ask me to interview the current boss, since he has nothing to do with the claim." I could hear how my words sounded as they rushed out, slightly angry, nervous. Javi went racing across the field after a crow.

"I'm not sure, either, but you know these claims adjusters are under a lot of stress and they just want to be assured that we know what we are doing. It's best just to do what the claims adjusters ask, and again, if you have any questions, contact me."

"Okay," I said. "Hey, I just want to make sure I'm doing a good job!" I laughed.

"I know you do," Josh said and we got off the phone.

My stomachache intensified. I surmised that, for different reasons, the claims adjuster and Josh wanted me to ask no questions and do as I was told. I scanned the park for a restroom. I ran after Javi, scooped him up along with our snacks, and rolled the stroller backwards up into the dank building. Javi smiled at me and waved his string cheese around as I again shit my brains out into the park toilet. I fumbled some slightly moist toilet paper off the padlocked roll and wiped my asshole until it bled. I was starting to wonder if this job was going to be worth it in the end.

As I waited for the stress claimant to get out of a meeting, I read a small, framed poem on the hallway wall. It was a poem about getting older, and wanting to play in a park across a bridge. It had something to do with accepting the compromises that come with responsibility. I snapped a pho-to of the poem with my phone and wondered if this was what I was currently experiencing, the compromises that come with making money, having a job. I was being asked to empathize more with the claims adjusters, our clients, who I'd likely never meet, than with the injured workers with whom, for the most part, I shared a similar work history and background, who I spent hours interviewing and listening to. In this particular case, I was in fact being asked to give a pass to fishy mistakes, just because, as Josh had said, the claims adjuster was "stressed out," while also getting ready to essentially interrogate this man in the meeting about his stress-related workers' comp claim. Standing there, I felt sick with my own with stress, knowing that in a few minutes I would be asking the claimant about his past mental health history and the DUI he received several years prior.

The meeting dispersed and the claimant strode out of the boardroom with a smile on his face. He was over six feet tall, dressed in a plaid shirt, blazer, and blue jeans with a large silver buckle. Mr. Brown reminded me of a younger, more handsome version of our then governor, John Kitzhaber. He shook my hand and sat across from me at the large shiny wooden table. I turned on the recorder and started the in-terview.

Mr. Brown had brought along a typed statement and I assured him that I would include it in the report. It turned out that the former boss was the root of all the stress. Mr.

Brown stated that his former supervisor would often use foul and insulting language and regularly berate and demean him in front of other coworkers. According to Mr. Brown, the former supervisor would also make insane statements and blatantly lie. He speculated this had been done "to mess with" him. I scribbled notes on my interview form as the story continued.

"I have been an engineer for over twenty years, and he would force me to do things that were just plain wrong—that didn't make any sense." He flipped through his notes. "He was also misappropriating funds and I can prove it."

I took the papers and glanced at them out of a sense of obligation. This was problematic; claimants often viewed me as an ally—someone to whom they could complain about their workplace's dysfunctional and even illegal goings-on. I wasn't this man's ally, a truth I never addressed. I said nothing, just nodded and continued the interview.

I discovered that he had experienced panic attacks as a result of the stress at his job and had eventually been told by his doctor to go on medical leave. Mr. Brown had missed more than six months of work. I did some quick math in my head. If his claim were denied, his employer (or rather, its insurance company) would save many, many thousands of dollars. As he continued telling his story, I noticed the bags under his eyes. He had been prescribed therapy, antidepressants, and antianxiety medications. His eyes were large and green and looked haunted, somehow. I asked him what his symptoms were, and he described feelings of anxiety and dread.

Because of my familiarity with Cushing's Disease and cortisol's effects on the body, I knew the man was withholding a lot of his physical symptoms.

"What other symptoms have you experienced? Physical symptoms like sweating, or shaking hands, trouble sleeping?" I asked. I often found myself asking for more information than was required to fill out my form. I did this mostly out of curiosity, but also because I'd noticed that the average person is lousy at advocating for themselves. I wondered if the claims adjuster would approve of me "leading the witness." I wondered if my ever-swelling empathy would be picked up on the recording device that was perched so neutrally on the table between us.

"I've lost nearly eighty pounds," Mr. Brown said.

I felt myself blink and say, "Whoah." I couldn't help but give the man a once-over. He was massive, and his belly did hang ever so slightly over his belt line, but it was extra skin, I saw now, not fat. I could imagine that he had once been a much larger man. A real cowboy, a man who enjoyed his beer and his sports. Now he looked like a survivor. His eyes had that edgy, brittle look that my father's had taken on when I was a child, when he had to work a graveyard shift as a strike breaker for the Fred Meyer warehouse because it was the only job he could find and he had seven children to support. "Have you ever experienced these symptoms before?" I asked.

He revealed that he'd been previously prescribed antidepressants "a few years ago." When I pressed him for details he told me that his parents had died a few years back, and that his son had been diagnosed with a serious learning disability. "I was under a lot of stress," he confessed, "and I took some meds for a while."

I muttered something about having also been treated for anxiety before. I could feel him watching me as I scribbled down notes.

I asked him about his employment history. Then I asked him if he'd ever been arrested or spent time in jail. He replied that he had never been arrested or been to jail. This, of course, was a lie. He had lied to me. It's an odd feeling when someone lies right to your face. I have a friend who has struggled with drug addiction in the past and when she was using she would deny that she had lost weight, and for a moment, I would believe her even though it was obvious she had lost at least thirty pounds since the last time I saw her.

But could I blame the claimant for lying? The claims adjuster had sent me an email before the interview telling me that he'd been arrested for driving drunk, a fact I saw as irrelevant to his claim. And now he was lying to my face about it. *But what if he wasn't lying?* I began to wonder. I couldn't help but feel a little paranoid about why I'd gotten this email in the first place. Wasn't this just a way for the claims adjuster to preemptively encourage me to be adversarial with Mr. Brown?

Or perhaps the claims adjuster was lying? I had no way of knowing, unless I wanted to go out of my way to run background checks on the claimants. The claims adjuster knew I wouldn't do that. Or perhaps the claims adjuster thought she and I were on the same page—that we both understood my job wasn't about getting at the truth, but about intimidation.

The truth was, Mr. Brown had already divulged the most damning evidence anyway. He'd been treated for depression and anxiety before. It could be considered a pre-existing condition.

I asked him why it had taken him so long to file his claim since he had been put on medical leave almost a year prior.

"Well, I knew the deadline was approaching!" he said and smiled.

My stomach sank. This guy was so naive. He had no idea who he was dealing with. The fact that he had waited so long could only hurt him. In fact, with so little time for his paperwork to get processed, the insurance company might see this as a golden opportunity to mess his case up. It all made a little more sense now. Perhaps this was why the dates had been so screwy for this claim. Was this why the claims adjuster seemed to willfully instruct me to interview the wrong boss? I had the sneaking suspicion that the claims adjuster was trying to gum up the whole process. If she could deny the claim based on a missed deadline, it would create more work and possibly the need for legal counsel on the part of the claimant. I took a deep breath. My stomach was turning over. I needed to wrap this up before I pooped my pants.

I went back over the interview, summarizing what he had told me, asking him again if he'd ever been arrested. Once again, he denied it. I read the closing statement and turned off the recorder.

As I gathered up my things, the man turned to me, his eyes wide and glassy. "Why are you guys asking me all these questions?" he asked. "Are you just looking for a reason to deny my claim?"

I felt my stomach turn again. I wanted to tell the man to get a lawyer. I wanted to tell him he was in way over his head. The recorder was off, no one would ever have to know. Instead, I gave him the line that Josh had given me for these situations. "My only job is to come and ask you these questions," I said. "I have no idea what will happen to your claim after we are done here." But I could hear my voice shake and I stammered a bit when I said it. I felt like a coward. "Good luck," was all I could muster at the end as I shook his hand.

On the drive home, I pulled off the road to take a call from my doctor. I had called her office the day before to ask about my chronic diarrhea. "I just started a new job," I said into my cell phone. "It could be stress-related."

The advice nurse didn't comment on this, she only relayed a message from my doctor: Take an over-the-counter antidiarrheal and drink plenty of water.

I was in the office writing up a report about a week later when Josh, Randy, and Ben, the head of surveillance, came into the room and set up chairs in front of the large TV screen in one corner of the room.

"Martha, it's not going to bother you if we have a business meeting right now, is it?" asked Josh.

"If it bothers me," I said, "I'll just put on my headphones."

Josh and the others commenced going through the numbers: the surveillance cases, different problems with technology, footage. They compared their numbers to the other offices around the country. Josh pointed out different categories in which the Portland office outperformed the competition.

I mostly ignored them until Josh asked me how the reports were going. I turned around in my chair and shrugged. "They're going fine," I said. But then I felt I had to bring up the question from Mr. Brown.

"I did have one claimant say to me—you know the guy from last week—after the interview was over, he asked, 'Are you guys just trying to find a reason to deny my claim?'"

I told them how I had responded. And then I waited.

Josh nodded. Randy and Ben stared blankly at me. And

THE END OF MY CAREER

then, as if I hadn't said a word, they turned back to their meeting and continued examining the numbers. I waited and waited until I realized there was going to be no response to what I had just said.

There was a lull in business. For the first time since starting at Marley & Marley, I had finished all my assignments and was waiting for new cases.

"They'll start coming in again, don't worry," Josh said over the phone. "We've all been slow. There's nothing on the surveillance side, either." It was September and Josh told me that it was probably because all the claims adjusters were on vacation.

He was right. About a week later, I got another case. I had never worked with this particular claims adjuster before. She used a term in her email to me that I didn't understand. I called Ben because Josh was unavailable. Ben couldn't define the term either, at least not in the way the claims adjuster had used it. He recommended that I call the claims adjuster and ask her. When I did, she treated me as if I were a moron. I listened patiently as she explained a bunch of stuff about workers' comp that I already understood, but never adequately defined the term in question. I realized that I would only make things worse if I asked her any more questions, so I just blankly said, "Yes, I understand," and got off the phone as quickly as I could.

Ten minutes later, Ben called me back. "The claims adjuster is upset," he said. "She is thinking about not using us now. What did you *say* to her?"

I sighed. "I didn't say anything. I run into this problem a lot. Just because I ask a lot of questions people think I'm a moron. I still don't know what she meant by that term and now she thinks I'm incompetent." I re-read him the claims adjuster's email and explained how it didn't make sense.

"Look," Ben said. "She's probably just stressed out. But I mean, to be honest, I don't even know what she meant by that."

Then Josh called me, and we had the same conversation. He told me that he also didn't know what the term meant in the context of the email. I wondered if Josh cared at all about his job, or what he was doing. I wondered if I was just smarter than him. Again, the underlying message seemed to be: *Don't ask questions. If you don't know what something means, pretend that you do. Inspire confidence even if you don't know what the fuck you are doing.* But I was never explicitly told any of this. I began to feel as if I were being punished for the very traits I was hired for.

That week I was housesitting at a beautiful old house in Corbett for the parents of a high school friend. It had been nice to stay out in the country in what felt like the last days of summer. Bernard and I invited my friends Tess and Mark over to dinner. After dinner in the garden, we moved inside and sat around the kitchen table. Tess leaned over and asked how the new job was going.

"I actually hate it!" I laughed bitterly.

"Wait, remind me. What are you doing again?"

I got about halfway through my explanation when Tess stopped me. "That's what Mark used to do!" she exclaimed.

I suddenly remembered that Mark had worked for some kind of evil medical insurance company many years ago, when he and Tess first started dating. After that he'd spent a while on unemployment and eventually went to grad school to get his degree in public health administration so he could help people get health insurance. He'd been instrumental in getting me enrolled with the Oregon Medical Insurance Pool (OMIP) when I had been kicked off my COBRA. (Before Obamacare went into effect, it had been virtually impossible for me to get private insurance because of my pre-existing conditions. OMIP was expensive but at least I had coverage.)

I'd known Tess and Mark for years, but when people describe their jobs, you never know what it is that they *really do.* I knew Tess was a family counselor, for example, but I didn't really know what she *did* every day.

"Wait, Mark was a private investigator?"

"No, he worked for a workers' comp insurance company."

I felt my head start to spin. "Mark. You did workers' comp? Who did you work for?"

"For a few years I did, for Initech."

"*What?!* That's one of our clients! Did you know that I am doing workers' comp investigations? I'm a private investigator!"

Mark took a drink of his wine. "Get out," he said. "Quit now."

It was like he had read my mind. "Yeah," I stammered, "I hate it. I kind of feel like my only function is to find reasons to deny people their claims."

Mark nodded. "That's because that is your only function. That is the *only* reason TPAs hire investigators."

Mark went on to describe his experiences at Initech. After college he landed an entry-level position and worked his way up to claims adjuster. "That's when I looked around and saw what was really going on."

He told me that when he was first promoted, he saw stacks of unfilled claims sitting on a desk. "I was like, 'Come on guys! We have to fill these claims!' But then I realized that they were all Hispanic names on the claims; one of the organizations we worked with was minor league baseball. The players came to the US to play baseball and then, of course, injured themselves. They were promised that they would be taken care of. But these were poor guys, baseball players from the Caribbean or wherever. They didn't speak English, so we, Initech I mean, knew they would never hire lawyers. So they never filled the claims."

My jaw dropped open.

He nodded and laughed bitterly. "I know! It was awful! In fact, I was given a script to read to people if they even mentioned the word 'lawyer.' If a claimant said 'Should I get a lawyer?' or 'I'm thinking about getting a lawyer,' I had this sheet of scripted lines that I was supposed to say: 'Why get a lawyer involved? We can work this out between the two of us. Lawyers only complicate matters' … stuff like that."

"Oh my god," was all I could say. It all made sense now. All the squirrelly answers from Josh, all the "mistakes" in the claims. And it was even worse than I'd feared.

"What did you do when you figured out what was going on? Did you quit?"

"Well, not exactly. I wanted the unemployment, so I basically got myself fired." Mark smiled. "I messed up other people's projects until they had to fire me!"

"Sabotage!" I laughed. "I don't think I could do that," I said, although the truth was that I'd just never had a job that paid me enough to make that worth my while. "But I really hate this job. I mean these people, the claimants, are like me: low-wage workers. And they are just getting screwed over. I'm too empathetic. I don't even know who would be good at this job. They hired me 'cause I'm a writer, but that's what writers do! We empathize. I've been having diarrhea for weeks from the stress!" My voice had gone up at least an octave.

Tess turned to me. "You of all people should *not* be doing this job."

Bernard chuckled uncomfortably. "I kept telling her not to quit," he said.

"Everyone has been telling me that," I said, putting my hand on his shoulder. "But you didn't really know how bad it is." I pointed across the table. "Mark knows what it's really like."

"Doing that job," Mark said, "I couldn't live with myself. Seeing all the unethical, and yes, illegal stuff that I saw."

"What should I do?"

"You know what you need to do," Mark said, taking another drink of his wine. "Quit."

"That's it," I said. "I'm going to quit." Immediately I felt a huge weight lift off my shoulders. "I'm going to quit tomorrow."

Mark and Tess laughed, surprised that I had made the decision so easily. "Congratulations!" said Tess. They both seemed delighted. Soon we said our goodbyes.

That night I couldn't fall asleep; I kept running through different scenarios in my head, what I would tell Josh the next day. I knew I would have to turn in all my files, my recorder, and my work laptop. By the time the clock struck 2:00 a.m. I had formulated a plan: In the morning, on my way to work for my mother, I would drop off my work-issued laptop and other electronics at the Marley & Marley office and resign.

I had already decided that I didn't want to come off as self-righteous. Quitting without notice was bad enough—what use was there in trying to make everyone feel bad about themselves? I came up with a statement, so to speak, and practiced it several times in my head before finally falling into a fitful sleep. I dreamed I was at a garden party where the guests were eating my body as if I were a roasted pig, laid out on a table surrounded by fruit and wilted lettuce, flies buzzing in and out of my ribcage.

In the morning, Bernard wished me luck and kissed me goodbye. I drove directly to the Marley & Marley office. I didn't see Josh's SUV in the parking lot. I was relieved because I was dreading having to see him, but my stomach was already in knots. The younger surveillance guy Ben pulled in on his motorcycle. I mumbled a hello.

"And I need to talk to you," I said as I followed him down the stairs and into the office he and Josh shared. I figured I might as well break the news to this guy, since he had been treating me as an inferior since he'd been transferred from California. "I'm quitting today," I said. "Here's my work computer and all my files."

"What happened?" He wore a look of concern. "Wait, let me call Josh."

"No, that's not necessary." I held up a hand, took a deep breath, and said what I had practiced last night. "I've always had jobs where I felt like I was helping people. And in this job I just feel like I'm helping insurance companies. I don't think I'm a good fit."

Ben frowned. "Yeah, I feel ya there." He reached for his cell phone. "Wait, let me call Josh."

"No," I shook my head. "There's really no need. I'm sorry but I just can't continue. I've made my decision. Thanks for all your help."

I turned and walked out of the office. I stopped in the hallway and stuck my head into Monica and Randy's office.

"Bye, guys," I announced. "Today is my last day. It was nice meeting you."

They both looked shocked. And that was a delicious moment. It's always nice to surprise people who think you are a moron by doing something they would never dream of doing themselves. I got in my car and drove to my mother's real estate office. I felt almost high with the relief of knowing I would never have to call another claimant ever again.

When I arrived at my mother's office, she congratulated me on doing the right thing. The receptionist at her office also congratulated me. My grandmother happened to call and I told her what I had done. She told me that I had done the right thing and that she would be praying for me. I felt more righteous by the minute.

Then I sat down to write Josh an email. I figured he deserved some kind of explanation:

Hello Josh,

As Ben may have already told you, I resigned today. I am very sorry that I wasn't able to put in a two-week notification with my resignation, but I had a sleepless night last night thinking about it, and to be honest I have felt conflicted with this job from the very beginning. After I made the decision at four in the morning, I knew I couldn't work another day doing the job of claims investigator. I have always had jobs where I felt like I was directly helping people. The problem with working for Marley & Marley is that I feel like I am really only helping the insurance companies. The actual job of interviewing claimants has been emotionally taxing and stressful, especially knowing that I may or may not be helping the insurance companies deny their claims. This was just not a good fit for my personality.

I have enjoyed getting to know you and everyone at Marley &
Marley. Thanks so much for having faith in me and showing
me the ropes.

Best of luck to you,
Martha

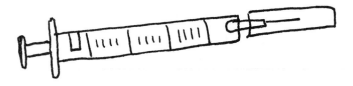

Hi Martha,

It pains me to see that you have been feeling this way since being
hired and didn't approach me about any of it. A statement is
part of the claims process and if nobody gets a statement from
the claimant, there is essentially no claim. I would say that the
majority of claimants we speak to are compensated favorably,
our job is to get their side of the story when they would otherwise
have no voice. As a third party we are actually doing them a
huge favor by providing an objective interview, instead of hav-
ing a biased claims adjuster be the one to interview them.

Sorry to see you go with this short of notice, and again I wish you would have communicated your issues before making your decision, but nonetheless good luck in your future endeavors.

Regards,
Josh

After reading his email, I felt a pang for a moment; was there a chance I'd been too hasty in believing Mark's version of events? But, on the other hand, Josh's email still missed the point. It didn't really matter to me if, as he claimed in his email, most of the claimants I interviewed would end up getting their workers' comp. What mattered was that I was being used as a tool of intimidation and suspicion. It also mattered that the cost–benefit analysis never quite penciled out for me; the insurance companies had to be denying a significant portion of the claimants I investigated in order for our service to be worth it to them.

What struck me most about this email exchange was how terribly insincere we were with one another. Aside from Josh, it hadn't been nice getting to know the crew at Marley & Marley. I had only stayed up until two in the morning, not four as I claimed in the email. I could see now that my attempt to not come off as deeply self-righteous had failed miserably.

On the other hand, I couldn't believe that Josh had never picked up on my doubts about the job. That he continually brushed my questions off was evidence of how deeply entrenched he'd become in the business of workers' comp claims; he couldn't see what was right in front of him. Or wouldn't.

I could see how his description of my role as a claims

investigator was soothing to him. Maybe he wasn't entirely wrong. Maybe I *had* helped some claimants. But I knew that a lot of the information I gathered could and would be used against them, and I no longer wanted anything to do with it. How could we work for the claimants and the insurance companies at the same time? It was an impossible situation. Again, I wondered if Josh was stupid. Meanwhile, he was probably thinking the same thing about me.

I never replied, even though I wanted to.

A few weeks later I went to my primary care doctor to see about getting a medical marijuana card. As a side note, I told her again about my IBS symptoms, how the stress of the job had kept me on the toilet for three months. I told her I'd already been given a two-year award for my disability. "I want to keep my options open for re-applying for disability in the future if I need to," I said. "So I wonder if a diagnosis of IBS would help me later on, to add to my symptom list."

My doctor turned to me. "Disability is really hard to get," she said. "You have to basically be missing an eye." She closed one eye for effect.

"Well, I've already received disability," I said, figuring she must not have heard me the first time.

"Yeah, I don't think you can get disability just for IBS. They don't give disability to just anyone. You have to be like missing an arm or something." And she swung one arm limply by her side.

I couldn't believe what I was hearing. Her clumsy pantomime made it even worse. It was as if she'd forgotten I was the same woman who had been coming into her office every other month for the last three years complaining about chronic pain, digestive issues, depression, anxiety, and every other health problem you could imagine. And hadn't she just heard that I had already been deemed disabled by the federal government? I'd heard horror stories from other chronically ill people about insensitive doctors and disbelieving behavior from medical professionals, and now I was experiencing it myself. In that moment, my doctor's response seemed so out of line with my reality that I wasn't sure if it had actually happened. Stunned, I said nothing as she finished up the paperwork for my medical marijuana card.

A week or so after I quit the PI job, it was my father's birthday. He was just getting back into the swing of things at work but was already wondering about when they were going to give him his van back. He told my mother and me that his employers were being evasive about it. On the way to meet him and my family for dinner, I stopped at a Target to get him an iTunes gift card. As is usual for me when I am stressed out about money, I hadn't been checking my bank account for a while; my income had been cut in half after quitting the PI job. After parking, I checked the balance on my phone and grinned. I had fifteen thousand dollars in my bank account. More money than I had ever had in my bank account in my entire life. It was bittersweet—having the money and knowing it represented three years of illness and pain and would barely cover my credit card debt. I went into the Target and bought my dad two gift cards.

Later that month, he came home from work and told me he'd been laid off. "Laid off?" I said.

"I feel like they fired me," he said. He looked tired.

"Did they give you a reason why?"

He set his lunch box down on the counter and took a water glass out of the cupboard. He shrugged, turning away from me and letting the water run until it was cold. "I think it has to do with my hand," he said into the sink.

The old Martha would have told him that they wouldn't do that, that his employers must know it had been an accident. But the new Martha was beginning to understand that being supportive often means being cynical. "I'm sure it was because of your hand," I said.

He just nodded and slowly drank his water. He looked like he was trying not to cry but I couldn't be sure. Loyalty is important to my father. I was reminded of the claimants who talked about never being late, about their history with a company.

"I worked there for ten years," he said.

"That sucks, Dad," I said and gave him a hug.

He still doesn't know why he was laid off.

For my part, I did see Josh again. One night about a year later, I stumbled across his profile on OkCupid. There was all this stuff on his page about how much he loved his dog and going to see live music. Before I blocked him, I found it odd and a little disconcerting to see that, in addition to "running his own business," he was really "feeling the Bern."

Just Looking for a Date

I WAS TWENTY-THREE. It was summer and I was in Chicago. I was newly skinny; going through a mysterious depression, I'd lost twenty pounds. I was celebrating my new status as an extra-thin person by wearing skintight tank tops and short skirts. I was in Chicago as a member of the Eugene, Oregon, slam poetry team.

On our second day in Chicago, I walked out of a hot dog shop with a group of poets and a youngish, very tall blond man matched my gait. This is a weird thing—when a very tall stranger matches your gait on a busy city street. I was immediately on guard.

"I was wondering if you would want to come into this alley with me and my friend," the young man said.

I stopped. I didn't see a friend anywhere.

He smiled at me.

"We're working on a photography project and I was wondering if you'd let my friend take pictures of you in this alley over there." He pointed vaguely in the opposite direction.

My friend, let my friend ... the words jumbled together.

"What will you be doing?" I asked.

He was still weirdly grinning. "Well I'll be … " and then he made the universal I'm-wacking-off gesture. He giggled, as if this was the funniest thing he'd ever done or said.

"What?! No! I'm not going into any alley with you!" I said. I was horrified and disgusted. And I was confused, because nothing like this had ever happened to me before. "Why are you asking me to do this?" I asked, meaning why me, of all the women in Chicago.

"Well. Your skirt," he shrugged. The answer was obvious to him.

I ran away, skirt blowing up in the wind, and caught up with the rest of the poets. Thinking about it later, I wondered: *Had I just been propositioned?*

For years, my body was just something to carry my brain around in. Now, I measure work by its ability to most efficiently extract value from my body and the exertions of my brain. I have to ask myself: *If I am moving, how much money do I make per hour from that movement? If the job requires energy, in the end, is the pay worth a portion of the limited time I have left on earth?*

I once went on a date with a man and he told me about how he'd had a male friend who'd been approached by an older woman at a bus stop when he was a teenager. She'd propositioned him for sex. "Fifty bucks for an orgasm," she'd said.

"What did he say?" I asked.

The friend had told the woman that he "wasn't a prostitute." As if that were a thing one was rather than a situation one might find oneself in. As if any human interaction didn't have the potential to also be transactional.

Back in my cheesemonger days, I peripherally knew a wealthy young couple who were starting a dairy farm in rural Washington. They emailed me one day with a proposition: They wanted me to milk their goats, twice a day, every day, in exchange for a low wage and free rent. They framed it as a great opportunity for me, as a way into the dairy industry. I was offended. I couldn't figure out how the position would benefit me in any way. I'd be totally trapped on the farm; it was cheese servitude as far as I was concerned. I turned them down and wished them luck.

I have read that nine out of ten sex workers would rather be doing something else. But that does mean that one sex worker enjoys her job.

I was twenty-nine and living in San Francisco. I was two hundred pounds and sick with Cushing's Disease. I was in the habit of wearing sweatpants, sweat-shirts, and stocking caps. I would of-ten walk with a cane. There has never been a time in my life when I cared less about my appearance. I was in the business of surviving, not looking nice. One day, I was leaning against a circuit box in the Mission District smoking a cigarette. It was about three in the af-ternoon. I stubbed out my smoke on the sidewalk and started down 16th toward the BART station.

An older man with a big belly came up beside me and matched my gait.

Again, I was immediately uneasy.

He nodded at me. "You working?"

I didn't know what he meant, so I just said the first thing that came into my head. "No, I'm going to get some donuts," I said, and ducked into a donut shop. The donut shop happened to be right there and everything in me just wanted to get away from this man.

Few things make me angrier than when I tell someone (usually a woman) that I clean houses for a living and they respond in disgust.

"I could never do that job. I could never clean toilets for a living," they say, lip curling.

And then I get angry. I fume. What they don't understand is that I don't clean toilets for a living. Actually—yes, that's part of what I do. But a lot of what I do is just making people feel less stressed-out. I help them feel relaxed and at peace. I am my own boss and I make good money.

Then I want to say to these ladies that I could never do *their* jobs. I could never teach college-level creative writing. I could never be a nurse. I could never work at a dentist's office. I couldn't ever run a nonprofit. Those jobs are boring and tedious and underpaid.

And then I feel ashamed. The truth is I could do their jobs and would do their jobs if circumstances were different. I just don't happen to do their jobs and why am I being put on the defensive for merely answering a simple question?

I bet nine out of ten housecleaners would rather be doing something else, but I am the exception. And you could probably say this about most things we do for money, that—as the saying goes—I wouldn't be doing it if they weren't paying me.

A couple of weeks ago, I went on Facebook and asked for women to share their stories of being propositioned on the street. I mentioned that I was writing an essay about sex work. A woman who had done sex work, someone I don't know, told me I had no right to write about it if I'd never done it. "You have all the privilege," she said.

I got defensive. I had the right to write about whatever the hell I wanted. No one was going to tell me what to do. Then I remembered *Nickel and Dimed*. How I'd hated that book. Barbara Ehrenreich had basically spent the whole book saying: "Cleaning houses is hard. Waiting tables is hard. Working at Walmart is hard." Yeah, no shit, Sherlock. People have told me that I wasn't the right audience for the book, which was certainly true. Maybe I was just angry that there was an audience for the book in the first place. That people didn't already know that, for most people, all work is drudgery.

The conversation on Facebook makes me wonder: *Am I really writing about sex work, or about sex and work? Or about the asking? The propositions themselves? Was a proposition a form of harassment? Was it fair to put it in the same category as the times men had groped me, grabbed me, yelled at me, and masturbated at me?*

No, it wasn't exactly the same. It certainly wasn't the same when I stopped asking myself *How dare they?* in regard to the men who wanted to have sex with me in exchange for money.

Maybe I was still asking why I, in particular, have been propositioned more than any other woman I'd ever met who wasn't actually a sex worker.

I was twenty-two, working at an Italian restaurant in Eugene. I was hosting that night with one of my sisters as my co-hostess. In addition to bussing the restaurant, we also waited on customers who sat at the cocktail tables. A short-haired, weaselly man in his thirties came in and sat down at one of the cocktail tables. I went over and started the routine, taking a drink order, chatting with him. He told me he was in town for work. I asked him what he did for a living. He told me he was in the film industry.

I brought him his drink and he gave me a twenty-dollar bill.

"Oh. Thanks!" I said and stuck the bill in my apron pocket. I was happy to get such a generous tip. Nothing like this had ever happened to me before.

He ordered a plate of caprese salad and a pasta dish and each time I returned to his table he gave me another twenty-dollar bill. When he'd reached sixty dollars, my delight began to turn to discomfort. There was something odd about his demeanor. He was humorless and sour-faced, more withdrawn than the pervy, jovial old men that I was used to waiting on at my last job at a diner.

I brought him another glass of wine and he handed me another twenty-dollar bill. I was now very uncomfortable. I found my sister where she was joking in the kitchen with the dishwashers. I whispered loudly, "That guy on table three has given us eighty dollars!"

My sister's eyes grew big. "What!? That's awesome!" She was happy because the two of us pooled tips.

"He's weird," I whined. "I don't want to go back to his table. Will you bring him the bill?"

"Are you kidding?" she said. "Go back out there!"

I meekly returned and set the man's bill down on his table. He slammed his hand down on the bill, and as I turned to leave I heard him say, "I've given you eighty dollars and now you won't even look me in the eye?" He sounded angry, like he'd been ripped off.

I hid in the kitchen until he left. The extra money I took home that night didn't seem worth my lingering stomach-ache.

As I write this on my lopsided futon mattress, I'm thinking about those eighty dollars. I've just watched a documentary about an online dating site that sets up older, wealthy men with young women called "sugar babies." The understanding is that the men will provide gifts, money, sometimes rent and even college loan payments for the companionship and sexual partnership of the young women. The documentary interviewed both the young women and the older men, sussing out their motivations, their fears, etc. I remember one of the sugar babies, a twenty-three-year-old college student, asking: "Why would I date someone my own age? At best, a college student like me could only pay for their own meal on a date, not mine, too. And what am I getting out of it?"

I have to ask myself: *Did I waste my youth on other youth? Should I have been chasing older, wealthy men?* At thirty-five I'm now past my prime, my body would fetch far less on the market of sexual desires than it would have at twenty-three. And dang it, now I'd missed my chance to get my college paid for. But then I remember that my aunt and uncle had paid for my undergrad anyway ... so what is my point?

Maybe I'm really wondering: *Had I squandered the pinnacle of my sexual power on the undeserving?*

I remember a cold bedroom, a young man I was dating, darting naked from my bed, one winter afternoon after we'd had sex.

"Think about how young we are," I'd said. "Think about how we'll never be this young again."

He had his back to me, and was taking a pee with the bathroom door open.

"We should try to be in our bodies as much as possible," I said.

I don't think he understood me. I don't think I myself knew what I meant. Maybe what I meant was that I wasn't really enjoying the sex.

I briefly dated a much older man when I was twenty-five. We met through a friend. He had a jealous streak and would often try to tell me what to wear. He once whispered in my ear how much he liked walking into a bar "with a beautiful woman" on his arm—how everyone looked at him with envy. What had I gotten out of the relationship? When I broke up with him, he told me I was a horrible human being.

I understand what these sugar babies are thinking: *If you are going to have bad sex, you might as well be paid for it.*

I tell my housecleaning clients there are things that are not part of my service, things I don't do: I don't pick up stuff off the ground. I don't make beds. I don't do laundry. I am a house*cleaner*, not a house*keeper*. I don't clean the insides of cupboards and closets. I don't wash windows. Although sometimes I will find myself doing these things—if I have extra time or energy. But I don't want them to expect it. That is the distinction. If I wash your windows or pick up your child's room before I vacuum, it's because I'm doing you a favor.

82nd Avenue has a reputation, but for most of my life I thought its reputation was just another way snotty Portlanders would disparage East Portland. I worked off 82nd for a few years, for my friend Taya at her jewelry studio.

One day at the studio I remarked on this. We were standing in front of the large windows that looked out onto 82nd Avenue. "Everyone always talks about all the prostitution on 82nd. I've never seen a prostitute," I said.

"There's one right now!" Taya laughed and pointed out the window at a woman walking along the sidewalk towards the studio.

The woman looked average to me, normal. She was wearing jeans and a T-shirt and carrying a small purse tucked under her arm. Her hair was pulled back in a neat ponytail. She was about forty, thin, and just slightly underdressed for the weather. I don't know what I'd been expecting—fishnets and a halter top?

"I see her out there all the time," Taya said. "She walks up and down. First one way and then back again. All day."

"That's how you know?"

"Yeah, because she's out there all the time, not going anywhere. Not looking like she's going anywhere. And she's always looking into the cars as they pass by.

"Yeah," Taya continued, "I turn my van around in a parking lot across the street because it's too hard to take a left at that intersection. Sometimes when I pull into the parking lot, women just start walking towards my van because they think I'm pulling in there to pick one of them up."

On the drive home that day I saw the same woman again, still walking up and down 82nd. We made eye contact as I passed her.

I used to walk aimlessly a lot, too, when I was younger. No big mystery there.

One morning in Portland in 2004, I was riding my bike at 5:00 a.m. to do cheese inventory at the grocery store. It was still dark out and a little cold. I was in a quiet residential neighborhood when a large white suburban came up behind me with its brights on and slowed way down, trailing me. There was plenty of room for the car to get around me, but after half a block it still hadn't passed, so I rode up onto the sidewalk and waited for it to drive by. The driver had both his windows down. Instead of driving past, he came to a stop next to me. I was on the right side, so as he spoke he leaned towards the passenger window.

"Where's Division Street?" he yelled.

Division Street was only a couple of blocks south of where we were. It was a stupid question. "It's just a couple blocks that way," I said, pointing. "You can't miss it."

He didn't move. "Come over to my window," he said.

I thought maybe I'd misunderstood him. "What?"

"Come over to my window," he said again.

My heart was now steadily thumping in my chest. I glanced around. The houses were dark, everyone was still in bed. It was deathly quiet. I'd heard that most kidnappings happen at this time of day, early in the morning so that it will be the end of the workday before your family knows you're gone.

"You need to leave now," I yelled.

The man just sat in his car and stared at me.

"Leave, or I'm gonna call the police!" I yelled, my voice shaky. I was bluffing; I didn't have a cell phone.

It worked, though. The man stepped on the gas and squealed away. Once I was sure he was gone, I rushed madly on my bike to the grocery store, my heart racing.

Later that day, when I told my friend Ledena about the white suburban, she was concerned. She'd been volunteering for the Portland Women's Crisis Line. She told me there was a registry for stories like this. "There is a list of sexual predators," she said. "Maybe if you report it to the police, they can get a description and put your story on the list."

I liked how that sounded, how even if nothing happened with this creep, I could add my information into the database and maybe it would help other women. This guy could be a serial rapist for all we knew.

They sent a police officer to my house the next day. I stood outside on the front porch and told the officer what had happened. He was serious, standing with his notepad, scribbling notes. But when I got to the part where I yelled at the man and he sped off, the officer grinned and put his notepad back in his pocket. "Maybe he was just looking for a date," he said.

Years later, when I told my grandpa the story about the man in the suburban, he chuckled. "Maybe he was just looking for a date," he said.

I couldn't understand why a story about me being scared for my life was funny to both the police officer and my own grandfather.

Just thinking about this story again makes my heart race. I get that itchy feeling in my muscles and my stomach hurts.

I'm an explainer. I want to explain it all to everyone so they will understand what it feels like, in your body, to be a woman, to be unsafe.

I consider the girl that I was, the woman I am: silly, sexual, vulnerable, angry, walking around like an open-faced sandwich most of the time. No headphones, no sunglasses, no walking straight ahead in a suit of invisible armor. I have always been walking around, making eye contact with strangers. Taking photos and daydreaming, drinking in the world.

A few weeks ago I had sex with a man. During the middle of it, he stopped and said, "Oh my god, you're bleeding everywhere."

There was a dark pool of blood on the blue sheets. I looked down at my hand; somehow I'd missed the blood all over my fingers.

We got in the shower. I couldn't stop laughing. He didn't think it was funny and seemed disturbed.

"I would have kept going," he said, "but I thought it would turn me into a serial killer or something."

"I haven't had a period in nearly a year," I said. "Maybe it's something to do with my IUD."

He looked like he wanted me to stop explaining. As if he didn't want to be reminded that I had a body.

We got back in bed. I came quietly. He kept going and then just starting ramming me. I found myself checking out.

"Did you come?" he wanted to know. I nodded.

"Do you want me to come?" he asked. I nodded.

The Five Stages

When I was small, my family rented an old dilapidated peach-colored house on 76th and Taylor in Southeast Portland. Back then, Montavilla was a working-class neighborhood. Since we only had one car, a red station wagon, and my mother stayed home with us, my father biked downtown to work. The blocks surrounding our house were filled with other families. A family fostered children on the corner, my aunt and two cousins rented a house across the street, then there was us in our peach house, and a few more families down the block.

Our house, however, had a mouse problem. The problem got so bad that eventually my mom borrowed my aunt Paula's cat Squeak because she'd been told that he was a good mouser. I remember standing in the kitchen with my mom and Squeak, all of us staring at a small gray mouse frozen in fear against the wall. Squeak waited at my mother's feet; he didn't seem to see the mouse. My mom encouraged him like you would a dog: "C'mon Squeak! Get the mouse!" She pointed at the mouse. But Squeak did nothing. Every few seconds the mouse would dart a few inches closer to safety and Squeak's head would jerk in reaction, but he wouldn't pounce. Eventually the mouse darted beneath the fridge, out of reach. My mother threw her hands up in disgust. "Stupid cat. He can only see the mouse when it moves!"

I am this cat.

Once upon a time there was a bar in Portland, on 28th and East Burnside, called the Hungry Tiger. It was one of those old Chinese restaurants with a pagoda-shaped sign that advertised "Chinese and American Food." I don't know how the food was; I went there to drink, often during the day while my laundry was drying next door at the abandoned-seeming laundromat. I was twenty-three, and new to Portland. On a hot day, after lugging my laundry down the street, sipping a gin and tonic alone in the cool, dark bar felt perfect. I also frequented the place with friends. I remember Aaron's shocked face when I told him I was dating a man fifteen years my senior. I remember helping Ledena and Casey kick a man who seemed to be having a psychotic episode out of the bar. The man ran out screaming, waving his skateboard around wildly in the hot summer night. One night Janet Weiss came in by herself, went to the poker machine, played a couple of games, and then abruptly left.

The Hungry Tiger was intimate, small, slightly dangerous. A place where a rock star could gamble anonymously and not realize the skinny white girl two booths over cleaned her toilet. See, at the time, I was Janet Weiss's housecleaner. Earlier that day I'd vacuumed the kitty litter from her bedroom floor and straightened her Henry Darger coffee table books, before mopping my way out of her house, as if I'd never been there.

That part of Portland is still peppered with dive bars. There is Holman's, where you can spin a wheel on the wall for a chance to win a free meal, and Beulahland, which used to be cash-only and a hangout for anti-racist skinheads but now is just a normal dive bar with torn vinyl seats and a regular DJ night. Down the block was another dive-y Chinese place called Chin Yen, where I happened to be sitting alone one night in 2008, chain-smoking with strangers, watching Obama become president. Chin Yen didn't survive his presidency.

When I lived in that area of Portland, I once looked at a map published online by the Portland Police Bureau showing crime in a ten-block radius surrounding my house. The greater the density of crimes, the redder the map. 28th Avenue was one long gash of crimson.

The Hungry Tiger and the laundromat were demolished in 2007. In place of the kitschy facade of the Chinese restaurant they built a tall, shiny condo with jutting balconies and right angles. I was disgruntled. Not only was the Hungry Tiger gone, but the aesthetics of the area were now muddled and incongruous. One night, a friend of a friend, a Midwest transplant who worked for the mayor's office, said flippantly in my presence, "I don't know why everyone is so upset that an ugly old dive bar is being torn down and replaced by something new."

Everyone else seemed unfazed by this comment.

But I looked at her as if for the first time. *Who is this strange being in my presence?* I wondered. *She is breathing, talking, laughing, a seemingly kind and loving person in service to my city, and yet she has no heart or human empathy or soul.* I had thought her simpatico, but I was obviously wrong. I felt I had misjudged not only her, but perhaps all of humanity.

Yes, the Hungry Tiger was an old dive bar. But the new building was ugly in its own way. Was this just a matter of aesthetics? Was I just upset because I didn't want change? She was right. The Hungry Tiger was ugly, but implied by her mostly rhetorical question was the assertion that I had no right to be upset. That I was being irrational and silly.

The Sandy River flows down from Mount Hood, loops around Larch Mountain and into the Columbia River, which churns west through Portland, picks up more water from the Willamette, and steadily widens until it reaches the Pacific Ocean at the town of Astoria.

I grew up on the Sandy, and my mother and aunt Paula used to live in Astoria. A branch of my family still owns a smoked fish shop there. The rain that falls here reaches the ocean there. It's all connected. And for a while that's how it was with the Sandy and me; there were no boundaries, no hierarchies, no jobs, no housing laws. When you live in a backwater, there's room for everyone.

Many times over the past decade, I've invited Portlanders down to a secret spot on the Sandy River. I thought nothing of it until my sister Ana, who uses the spot much more than I do, told me to stop bringing people out there.

"Especially people from Portland!" she hissed. I thought she was being paranoid. Besides, I was "people from Portland." What did she have against us?

I couldn't think of anywhere that I liked better than Portland. Drier climates seemed dead or dying. The weather in other places was too hot or too cold or too the-same-all-the-time. There were hurricanes, violence, Republicans, and poverty in other places. If a city was more crowded than Portland, I found it stressful. If it was less crowded, it seemed boring. Sure, I'd had friends who'd moved to Los Angeles to pursue acting, or New York to launch their careers in the publishing industry, but I'd never felt the need to move away, mostly because nowhere else seemed any better, and in fact other places were mostly worse. The Sandy River *was* Portland just as I was the Sandy and I was Portland and I was Oregon and I was the five acres I grew up on.

In 1999, the year after I graduated high school, my friend's father cofounded a local grocery store chain called New Seasons. When I moved to Portland after college, this friend helped me get a job at the new store being built on Division Street. At the time, she lived with a bunch of our friends in an old house right next to the construction zone. The house would eventually be jacked up and moved around the corner to a different lot, where it was turned into a Thai restaurant. But, for a year, my friends lived in this large, nearly empty house for free.

I visited one day, bringing bread pudding with whiskey sauce to share from my job at the diner in Troutdale. To my surprise, they weren't exactly happy about their situation; the arrival of the grocery store was met with hostility, as people feared it would raise rents and gentrify the neighborhood. My friend felt uncomfortable and on edge. She told me that one morning someone had spray-painted a huge sign outside the house with the words "Go Home New Seasons" or "New Seasons Ruins Neighborhoods" or something like that on it.

I'm not one to judge people's emotions as being good, bad, or even justified. That's not what emotions are. Did New Seasons cause rents to rise? I didn't know, I was just happy to have a job that provided health insurance.

For the next few years, after work, I often walked the couple of blocks up to the Red and Black Cafe to get a cup of coffee and smoke a cigarette outside. The anarchist café was run as a collective and served hippie fare: bowls of brown rice with broccoli, tempeh, and peanut sauce, the kind of food I was used to eating, having already lived in Eugene for three years. The café was a little dingy and even had its own weather system, as the large windows and high ceiling caused humidity and condensation. I overheard a lot of talk at the café about how New Seasons and the new Starbucks were ruining the neighborhood, and that it was just a matter of time before everyone was going to have their rents raised.

A block from the Red and Black, my father did electrical work on the new Starbucks. Not long after completion of the Starbucks, a vandal attempted to throw a Molotov cocktail through the window. It didn't work; the front window was made of reinforced glass. My father asked, "Why would anyone want to destroy a Starbucks?" He laughed, as if it were the most ridiculous thing he'd ever heard.

Back then I could reach everywhere in my world within thirty minutes. I walked to work and it took half an hour. I drove to my parents' place in Gresham and it took half an hour. Across town, half an hour. But when I gave up my car and had to ride the bus out to my parents' house, it took almost an hour. It was depressing. I felt poor. I felt as if my standard of living had taken a significant hit.

Maybe I am poor, I thought. I pushed the thought away. How could I be poor? I never had to worry about paying my bills.

I didn't know what money was. I didn't know that getting into the middle class was something to do. I knew about class insofar as I hated rich people. But the truth was that I didn't know any rich people. The closest I knew were upper-middle-class people.

I was young. I took my body and the city for granted. I hadn't yet encountered or internalized metaphors of any value in relation to the city; it wasn't an organism, it wasn't an ant nest, a beehive, a stand-in spouse, a heart beating inside the state of Oregon, a historical moment, an unsustainable aspect of civilization.

The Doug Fir Lounge and Jupiter Hotel opened in 2004. Ledena and I had just moved into a two-story teal-colored duplex on Burnside that we could barely afford. The place was drafty and spacious and we took on a third roommate, a musician who lived in the laundry room for two hundred dollars a month.

A woman named Shelly lived above us. We'd already heard from the previous tenants that Shelly was an alcoholic and wouldn't call the cops or complain if we had loud parties. So we did have many loud parties; with businesses on either side of us and Shelly above us, no one said a word. It seemed like the perfect setup.

There was a homeless man who would periodically sleep in an old camper in our backyard. He would hack and cough all night long outside my bedroom window. I was dating a boy who was allergic to feathers and we would shiver our skinny bodies together in my bed underneath my one blanket, with no pillows or comforter in the dark drafty house and I would think, *I feel you, man, you must be cold, too.*

Of course it wasn't like that at all—I hadn't the foggiest notion how he felt, and when we told our landlady about him, he screamed at her, called her a cunt, and told her that

Shelly had given him permission to sleep in the camper. That was the end of the camper. One night we were having a party and an intoxicated homeless woman came into our backyard. I watched as she violently tried to separate some male guests from the beers in their hands. Her eyes were blank and she was so drunk she couldn't speak. Some of the boys finally got her to leave.

The first time I met Shelly, she knocked on our front door and asked me to give her a ride to the emergency room because she felt "awful all over." She said she'd felt that way before and just needed some Vicodin. I gave her a ride. It turned out she was the ex-daughter-in-law of the landlords. They'd been letting her live there rent-free for years because they felt guilty kicking her out.

About six months after Ledena and I moved in, the landlords finally reached the end of their rope with Shelly.

They told us they were evicting her and had given her proper notice. Thirty days to pack up her stuff and leave. Not knowing anything about her situation, we expected her to start moving out. We knew she had some kind of social life; male friends would visit every so often. Of course, I'd also seen her at three o'clock in the morning, struggling for fifteen minutes to unlock her door, so drunk she could barely stand, her long blond hair swaying in counterpoint to her hips.

We naively thought she had someone to help her.

But no one arrived to help, and one day Shelly was gone. The day after she was evicted, I was leaving my apartment when a middle-aged man walked onto the porch. He held a single cardboard box. "Is Shelly here?"

"She was evicted yesterday."

"Yesterday?" he smirked at me. "I was supposed to help

her move!" He shrugged and stepped back down onto the sidewalk without breaking eye contact. "Well, if you see her, tell her Don said hi."

I nodded. *Shelly has shitty friends,* I thought.

The landlord's wife started cleaning out Shelly's apartment several days later. One afternoon, she invited me upstairs to see "the mess" that Shelly had left for them to clean up. I walked up the stairs to Shelly's apartment and

immediately felt queasy. Along the stairwell wall were empty wooden picture frames staple-gunned to the wall. Inside the frames were pages ripped from porn magazines, tacked haphazardly to the wall.

All the while, the landlord's wife was jabbering away about all the work she had to do, how messy and disgusting Shelly was. We reached the top of the stairs, and I saw she wasn't exaggerating. Trash was everywhere. All over the kitchen floor and counters. There were at least two hundred empty Pabst cans in view, on the floor, in a big pile in the sink. The stovetop was burned black, the wall behind the stove black too, in several different streaks, as if Shelly had caught it on fire several times over the years. I took it all in. We'd had no idea what Shelly was up to, risking total destruction of our home and lives, right there in that kitchen over our heads.

The only room that was in a state of near-order was her twin daughters' room. The room was still set up as if the girls lived with her. Their pink handprints were all over the green walls. Someone had painted pink roses and green vines around the windows and doorway.

"Look at this," the landlord's wife spat, "she left everything here!" She pointed at the stacks of photo albums and toys in random piles on the floor. Shelly had lost custody of her daughters years ago. The swing set in our backyard was rusting in the weeds. A few months earlier, on Christmas, I'd arrived home just as Shelly was giving her nervous-seeming daughters a cardboard box of wrapped gifts on the front porch. The girls stood close to their father. No one was smiling.

There in her empty apartment, I realized Shelly had probably been doing sex work to feed herself; the porn on the walls as well as the random male guests led me to suspect as much.

But only now do I understand how disingenuous the landlord's shock was, that Shelly had abandoned her belongings. They must have known that she was going to end up homeless. They knew she didn't have anywhere else to go. This was why they'd waited until spring to kick her out. They were ruthless, but didn't want to feel guilty.

A few months later, Ledena saw Shelly sleeping under a bush on Ankeny, a few blocks from our house.

When the Doug Fir opened that year, I hadn't seen anything like it before. My coolest friend Emily told me our friend Nathan had already gotten a job there waiting tables. We were both a little jealous; jobs were hard to come by in Portland those days, especially cool jobs. Not long after it opened, I went to a Talkdemonic show to see the place for myself. I was dazzled by the design, the cleanliness, the great sound in the venue downstairs, the hip glass and gold accents, the newness of it. Something cool had arrived in our neighborhood.

As I was walking outside during the break to have a smoke, I noticed a blond girl a few years younger than me sitting on the vinyl bench by the door. She caught my eye because we were both wearing the exact same thing: a vintage black leather motorcycle jacket with white leather lining. Hers, however, was in much better condition. I felt upstaged.

By the time I arrived in Portland, the Pearl District had already been "ruined." It didn't matter to me that artists had been forced out of their cheap warehouse lofts; the change had happened before my time, it was on the other side of the river, I never went there, and I didn't know any of those people. My friend dated someone who lived in the Pearl, a software developer who had moved here from somewhere else. We made fun of him and called him a yuppie behind his back.

As my twenties rolled by and I stayed in Southeast, my friends began moving to North Portland into predominantly black neighborhoods. I stayed behind so I could walk to work. They talked about feeling weird, being the white newcomers, outsiders. The gentrifiers. I felt bad for the black community in Portland. But not bad enough to do anything about it. What could be done? The way it was talked about, in the media and among people I knew … it seemed like the natural course of events, like it was inevitable. Besides, my friends weren't trying to displace anyone. They were just looking for cheap rent.

Who could blame them for that?

One day at New Seasons, bored out of my mind, I counted the customers who weren't white coming into the store. Over the course of my shift, the number was in the low teens. I told a coworker about it and she seemed horrified. Like I was a racist for trying to pass the time. My point was that the neighborhood near Ladd's Addition had always been pretty white, not to mention the rest of Oregon, but lately, it had seemed *really* white. Hadn't she noticed it—how the neighborhood was changing? The clientele seemed more affluent, more PC, more liberal … more of everything, really. One Halloween, my coworker who'd dressed up as a pirate was cornered by a customer, a white woman in yoga pants, her basket filled with expensive vegetables. "Pirates are real and they kill people!" she scolded him. "It's not funny!" She may have even complained to the management about his costume.

I got on Craigslist one night and looked at rentals in my neighborhood and I realized my apartment was on the extremely cheap side. I'd always known it was a good deal, but now I felt incredibly lucky. "Blessed," even.

I felt grateful. *What a luxurious life I lead,* I would often think, sitting in my apartment with a bottle of wine and a hunk of gourmet cheese that I'd gotten for free. *People who complain about their circumstances should know that it's the simple things in life that make it worth living.* That's what I would think, as I sat and enjoyed my cheese in my two-bedroom apartment that I rented by myself for $480 a month, all utilities included, on 24th and Hawthorne.

In 2011, when I returned to Portland from grad school, I moved in with my boyfriend John two blocks off Division Street. The changes to the neighborhood seemed to have accelerated while I was gone; Pok Pok, the Thai street food place, was now nationally known, and opening a branch in New York City. Stumptown Coffee was selling out to investors and had a branch in, yes, New York City. New condos and businesses were popping up all along the street.

John thought it was spectacular; he was a major foodie, and the owner and chef of his own food cart. Everything he loved was now within walking distance of his house.

I went to a party, a book release for my friend. It was one of the first parties I'd been to since I'd moved back to Portland. Outside, people milled around and smoked cigarettes. I was off to the side, by myself, and I eavesdropped on a conversation two young men were having by the back door.

One of the men toed a wild chamomile plant with his sneaker. "I'm visiting my sister," he said. "I live in Phoenix. How long have you been in Portland?"

"Six months."

I noticed how both men stood, their feet pointing in two different directions, their arms noncommittal.

"How do you like it?" the visitor asked. "It seems like a pretty rad town."

"I do like it. Portland's pretty cool." The second man paused, and squinted off into the distance. "I'd say Portland is a five-year city."

The other man nodded and made no comment.

I became intensely irritated. I knew that I had to either walk away or say something aggressive. I stubbed out my cigarette and went back inside.

That spring, John's cousin Kristina visited us from New York and told us she was thinking about moving to Portland, or at least renting a house in the neighborhood. She stayed with us for a week or so while looking for a place. One day while we were out walking, she complained that she was being outbid left and right by "couples from New York." She'd lost one house off Division to a couple who'd paid a whole year's rent in advance.

If even an extremely wealthy person can't find a place to live in this neighborhood, I wondered, *how does anyone of modest means stand a chance?*

"You could live east of 82nd," I suggested. "A lot of people knock East County, but it's really not that bad."

"Her family lives there," John said to his cousin, under his breath.

I rolled my eyes. What right did John and his cousin have to make judgments about Portland? They weren't even from Portland.

Something new was going on here, and I wasn't sure I liked it. I felt like I was a firsthand witness to top-down economic pressure.

John's cousin eventually did find a place off Powell Boulevard near a Starbucks and a paycheck lender. I thought it was a kind of boring, nondescript house and couldn't understand why a person with her resources would settle for something like that. But as it turned out, she wasn't *actually* moving to Portland. The house was just a place for her to crash when she visited, and most of the time it remained empty.

Although there are a multitude of reasons why John and I broke up, I can trace our breakup back to the day I refused to pick up a baby gray squirrel that one of his cats had dragged into the house and was torturing in the corner of the dining room.

I had just moved into the house a month earlier, and John wasn't home. Watching his tubby gray cat swatting at the tiny, frightened rodent totally freaked me out. I called John on my cell phone and breathlessly told him, "The cats are torturing a baby squirrel! I don't know what to do!"

He arrived, angry. Annoyed that I hadn't handled the situation myself. He went directly to the squirrel, picked it up in his bare hands, and cradled the frightened animal.

"You don't understand," I said. "There's no way I would EVER pick up a wild rodent!"

From his sympathetic expression it was clear that he understood my misgivings, but I worried that I'd instantly become one of *those* people to him—a person who wouldn't rescue a baby squirrel, a person who didn't care about animals.

As it turned out, this wasn't the first baby squirrel that John's cats had caught. Years earlier, before we were dating, his cats had caught two baby squirrels and he'd rescued them.

John called the local Audubon Society and asked if they would take the infant squirrels. They refused, because it turned out the squirrels were eastern gray squirrels—an invasive species in Oregon.

John had scoffed at this designation. Why did it matter at this point? The native species, the western gray squirrel, was obviously not succeeding. The eastern gray was dominant. So why not protect it equally, as it was already, inevitably, irreversibly, here to stay? And so he'd set up a whole room in his house with branches and nuts and raised the squirrels—a female and a male—to adulthood.

I took it personally that John would favor a non-native species at the expense of our native western gray squirrels (never mind that I'd never seen a single one). I felt this was proof that he was one of *those* kinds of people. The kind of person who didn't value what I value. What do I value? Sticking up for the under-squirrel. Yes. I always stick up for the under-squirrel, especially if it is a native under-squirrel.

But really, I wasn't so sure of myself then as I now make myself seem. I wrestled with the conundrum. Do we fight the good fight against insurmountable odds, or do we accept the status quo, or at least accept the new status quo? I couldn't decide if John was just more realistic than me. Maybe he was right; maybe I should just accept things as they were and not try to return to an imagined golden age where everything was perfect and the western gray roamed free.

But perhaps if he'd been raised in Oregon he would've behaved differently.

After Division Street was altered beyond recognition, no one talked about how New Seasons had supposedly ruined the neighborhood; it was obvious that larger forces were at work. Besides, I had worked for the company long enough to know that they weren't stupid; they didn't choose locations at random, hoping people with money would just magically appear and shop at their stores. No, they did their homework and followed the money. Not the other way around.

The Red and Black Cafe was right on one account—they did have their rent raised. Their old space is now a wine bar. The Starbucks was eventually shuttered as well, not because of a rent increase but on account of a number cruncher at Starbucks headquarters determining that the store wasn't profitable enough. A local chain specializing in gourmet salads has taken over.

I haven't been to the Doug Fir in ages. The shows are too expensive and having drinks there usually involves navigating a sea of dudebros.

I had to Google what used to be at the site of the Doug Fir before it opened. It was a motel built in the '60s. It's odd how you forget almost immediately what used to be, as fast as it slides past your eyes, unnoticed from your moving car; the shifting baseline begins the day you are born into the city.

Recently, my sister Zoe was a bridesmaid in a wedding in the small town, Corbett, where we grew up. She came over to my parents' house on her way home. We chatted on the sofa and she told me that everyone at the wedding was complaining about "Portland People."

Zoe took a sip of her water and then gestured with her other hand, chopping the air. "They kept going on and on about it. Portland People, Portland People! I don't even go into the city anymore! They all move here from somewhere else and they want to change this and that. And they're not even from here!"

I grunted in response. I could see what they meant. At the same time I also felt like they were talking about me. Those Portland People. My Portland People. I'm Portland People.

"None of them are from here," I agreed.

The friends who had moved with me to Portland from Eugene after we graduated from college were from all over the country, but I didn't care; they were my friends. We were moving to Portland together, en masse. To implicate them would implicate myself. Even though I could have played the Oregon native card at any point in the last thirteen years, it had never seemed fair to do so. But the more I thought about the new batch of people moving to Portland, the more the city seemed to change, the more I felt my Oregon native card itching in my back pocket. I recognized the foolishness of my selective rage. But the rage itself, the fact that I was beginning to feel like an endangered species, was stronger than logic.

Zoe kept talking. She told me about how one of her law school colleagues had been eating a handful of hazelnuts in front of her the other day. "The true Oregonians," he informed her, "call these filberts."

She rolled her eyes. "I told him, 'I've lived here my whole life and I call them hazelnuts.' And he said, 'Yeah, but are you a real Oregonian?' And I said, 'Yes. Like I just said, I've lived here my whole life and I've always called them hazelnuts.' And he just kept going on and on about filberts." Zoe paused. "I'm just so sick of people who aren't from here telling me what Oregon is like!"

I was in grad school in San Francisco when the TV show *Portlandia* aired. At first I thought it was hysterical.

And then in one skit, one of the characters mispronounced "Willamette." For a moment I thought it was a sincere mistake—they just didn't do their research and no one in cast or crew knew or cared enough to correct them. But how could that be true? This was a show about Portland and you're going to mispronounce the name of the river that runs through the center of the city? I got angry. I imagined Fred Armisen scheming about this. I imagined him laughing at all of us True Oregonians for being so sensitive. Because that had been the whole point. To make us angry.

I watched the skit about the bicycle messenger with the ear plugs complaining about the ruination of a bar by the square dude. I wondered if the bicycle messenger was supposed to be hip? He didn't look hip. Maybe that was the point. Even the skits about the feminist bookstore started to get on my nerves. Good comedy is supposed to punch up, not down. I decided I hated the show.

Wandering around a craft fair one winter, I couldn't find anything I wanted to buy. Everything was wooden and had antlers on it. I finally found a bumper sticker for five bucks, and I slapped it on my 1995 Honda Accord. In the clunky script of the *Oregon Trail* computer game it read: "You have died of dysentery."

One summer, my friends Camille, Yael, and I went down to the Sandy River to my secret spot. A man began to swim across the river from the opposite bank. From where we were sitting we could see the parking lot and the fence that he'd climbed over to get to the river from another part of Oxbow Park.

He was a few yards away when he hollered, "Hey! How'd you guys get to that beach? Did you swim over?"

Before my friends could reply I yelled back, "I'm not going to tell you!"

"What?" He looked confused.

"I said, 'I'm not going to tell you!' It's a secret!" I heard Camille and Yael giggle nervously behind me.

The man scowled at me from the water. "That's the last time I ask you for any help!"

I felt my face turn bright red. I don't like confrontation. On the other hand, I found his statement ridiculous; of course it would be the last time he ever asked me for help, because he'd probably never see me again.

Camille smiled at me. I think she may have said something about me having a lot of guts. I also felt silly, as if refusing to disclose the directions to one dude was going to keep this spot from being ruined.

"You can find this place on Google Maps," I shrugged. And then I muttered under my breath, "I don't owe him anything."

That same summer my mom asked me to become her real estate partner. I decided reluctantly that getting my real estate license was not so horrible an idea after all. Mom bought me the materials and I started studying for the state and federal tests. Unfortunately it was incredibly boring, so I would put it off. I tried to complain to her about it, but she would just shrug and say she knew it was boring but that I should just plow through it.

Months went by with little progress. Mom thought maybe I had ADHD. Or at least ADD. I got some Ritalin. I thought the Ritalin would be a magic pill that made everything interesting. But it made me sweat and have headaches and body aches. I was bitterly disappointed that this must mean I didn't actually have ADD. I wondered if real estate was something I even wanted to do.

I would have much rather continued cleaning houses. I came very close to telling my mom that I just couldn't do real estate with her. I thought about it while cleaning houses. I thought about it while driving to my boyfriend's house. I didn't want to be a real estate agent. It was boring. Realtors were fake. They cared only about money. They fake-tanned and bleached their teeth and hair. I wasn't fake.

On the other hand, I could only clean houses for four hours a day before I was sore and tired. I imagined myself older, I imagined myself old, and still cleaning houses. That seemed an awful future.

But at that time things were going pretty well with cleaning houses. And more and more of my friends owned houses. Those lucky enough to buy before 2014 even had nice houses in nice neighborhoods. I cleaned for them and they referred me to their friends. I straightened up their houses and thought about studying for my real estate exam and how awful it was. I thought again and again about how maybe I wouldn't do it. I cleaned their bathrooms and thought about how my life would be so much simpler and less stressful if I just continued cleaning houses. Why couldn't my life be like it used to be? Why couldn't I live in an apartment on Hawthorne by myself, and walk to work, and work part time, and save my energy for my art and my writing?

But every once in a while, when I was cleaning a friend's house, I would pick up the same issue of the University of Oregon alumni magazine that I had thrown onto the floor of my Honda, and I would place theirs in the bathroom magazine rack, and I would feel horrible about cleaning houses. I knew if I continued to clean houses, and if my health didn't improve, I would never be able to move out of my parents' house.

Late last year, I dreamed that the Sandy River had run dry. My sister Ana groaned when I told her about it. "Awful," she said. In the summer she takes her kids there to swim and have a picnic at least two or three days a week. To both of us, the disappearance of the Sandy sounded like the worst possible thing, like the end of the world.

The last day I'd spent there had been worrisome; I found a big pile of trash that someone had dumped at the top of the trailhead. And when I got down to the river, I was dismayed again. Usually at that time of year, the river is low from lack of rain. But on that last visit in September, it was high and green, meaning the river was mostly glacier-fed from Mount Hood. Meaning the weather was unseasonably hot and too much snow was melting. (When the water is brown it means that heavy rain is feeding the river. Green means mineral-rich glacier water. Anything in between is a combination of the two.)

And then later that week, on the way home from Portland, I noticed Mount Hood looked bare. My parents, lifelong Oregonians, said they'd never seen the mountain so brown. There was hardly any snow to be seen. I thought, *We can still say that the pace of change is "glacial" but it no longer means what it used to mean; now it means that things are disappearing at an alarming rate.*

My book club decided to read a book called *The Sixth Extinction.* I joked that it should be called *Everything Is Fucked.* The first chapter was about the mass extinction of amphibians. The second chapter was about the concept of extinction itself. All the frog talk brought up memories of my childhood in Corbett. I remembered finding newts, frogs, and crawdads in the streams and creek that ran through our property.

The newts were fascinating to me. They were so pale and Gollum-like. As if they never saw the sun, their eyes small and squinty. The newts had only two modes of being: They would dumbly sit there as we poked them with a stick, or they would shoot away under a log, their long spines whipping furiously back and forth.

Crawdads were like the opposite of newts. Instead of porous white flesh, crawdads wore crimson armor. They were the Rip Van Winkles of the forest, grouchy old men rising from slumber after millions of years. Even as a kid I understood that crawdads must have descended from lobsters, but that they shrank and became shriveled and vicious over the years. They were refugees from the ancient ocean, washed up in a mountainside creek.

The West Coast of the United States has some of the biggest trees in the world. They're truly giant. Jurassic-seeming. Nearly all of them are gone now. Young forests are easier and more profitable to log.

Anyone who grew up in Oregon has seen the black-and-white photos of loggers posing before they bring down a really impressive tree. The loggers themselves provide a sense of scale. Saws and axes in hand, they stand impatiently in a wedge, a gaping mouth-shaped hole, in a cedar or Douglas fir. I imagine them pausing just long enough to grimly humor the photographer before getting on with destruction as usual.

One spring day I decided to visit the Ancient Forest in Oxbow Park for the first time as an adult. I'd only been there once before, when I was eleven, and I remember being in awe of the enormous trees. I got into my car and drove through farmland and down into the forest near the Sandy River. I paid the five-dollar entrance fee and started through the woods leading into the Ancient Forest. It was beautiful in that FernGully, fairy-tale kind of way that only Pacific Northwest forests can achieve. Moss and huckleberry and ferns dripped from every branch and fallen log. As many hues of green as you can possibly imagine. But I began to wonder if maybe I wasn't in the right spot. Where were the

THE END OF MY CAREER

giant trees? I pulled out the map, and lo and behold I was smack dab in the middle of the "old growth" portion of the park. Scattered everywhere in the forest were rotting, molten stumps. Even in their half-dissolved state they were still larger in diameter than any of the "new" trees. These ghost trees were the true ancient trees and they were gone forever.

I recently discovered that my cell phone's GPS app mispronounces Flavel Street; instead of "Flawvell," it robots out "Flayvill." I laughed bitterly. I wondered, what with all the newcomers in Portland, when the gMaps pronunciation will overtake the Portlander pronunciation. I already feel like an old timer because I can't help but refer to César Chávez Avenue as "39th." My grandfather still calls Martin Luther King Jr. Boulevard "Union Avenue" out of habit.

I have a friend named TJ who spent nearly a year teaching English in Xi'an, China. All year we sent letters back and forth about our respective lives in Portland and Xi'an. I received the following letter in May 2015.

Dear Martha,

I want to tell you about the changes to this city.

Four years ago the apartment building being built across from campus wasn't there. Four years ago everything around the campus was fields and farms. Four years ago the roads out to the college weren't even paved. Though it's already crumbling, the college I work at is only ten years old. Now there are factories and industrial parks all around campus and more going up in every direction. Down the road there are ten more apartment towers going up. No one is living in them yet and at night they look like a huge row of black obelisks.

The high-speed train station, where I catch the subway into the city, didn't exist four years ago.

I've learned a lot of this by talking to the other foreign teacher here.

I live at the north edge of the city, but not for long, the city is pushing out. The fields are being cut into huge lots and walled up for future development.

Xi'an is surrounded by a series of concentric ring roads; it can take an hour to go from one end of the city to the other end on one of the outer rings. A few weeks ago I took a bus from campus, taking one of the rings, making my way into the heart of the city, and it all looks the same out here: construction. More factories, more shopping malls, more apartment towers. At one point I saw twenty identical apartment towers being built in two rows.

Much has been made of China's 'ghost cities,' Ordos is an extreme example, but building so much makes sense. In the last decade China has seen a huge explosion of the middle class, millions of people are moving in from the countryside to the cities, the country is in the midst of a massive migration. There needs to be more places to live in the cities. A lot more. There are definitely hundreds if not a few thousand new apartment buildings going up in Xi'an.

My Starbucks (I am now a person with a Starbucks ... which is located in the same shopping mall as my Walmart) is in an area called Fung Chung Wu Lu. Four years ago there was nothing there, now it's full of office buildings, apartments, and shopping malls. The construction in this area is not slowing down either. Every day migrant workers from the countryside gather at the corner down the street from Starbucks waiting for work. These men and women, all middle-aged or older, sit on the street with paintbrushes and tools, dressed in everyday clothes, waiting for someone to drive up and hand them a hard-hat, to give them some simple but backbreaking job. The younger generations walk by with designer clothes and shopping bags, drinking coffee, and talking on their smart phones.

But not all this growth is pushing the city out; old parts of the city are torn down to make way for new buildings. There are parts of Xi'an that my students call 'villages in the city,' streets and alleys with old houses and shops, which feel like you have walked into 'old China.' These places are making way for more apartments, more shopping malls. Beijing is famous for these alleys, called 'hutongs,' which have existed for hundreds of years and are disappearing as well.

While Portland wrings its hands as it figures out what it is becoming, Xi'an only marches forward to some glorious imagined future. If there is any second-guessing here, I cannot see it as an outsider. I wonder if the infrastructure will be able to handle a million more apartments switching on their power and water. I wonder if the roads can handle a million more cars. I wonder if they'll put up another power plant. There is a coal power plant ten miles from my school; I pass it on the way to the airport. They are building apartments right next to it. As the weather gets warmer here the air quality seems to be going down. I take allergy pills when I go into the city because the pollution upsets my sinuses.

Sometimes I walk by finished apartments with empty units and luxury shopping malls with stores but no customers. What if the people don't come? What if the housing market collapses like it did back in America? What if the economy slows down and people can't afford to move to the city? Has anyone decided that there is a limit to how much growth Xi'an needs? It's familiar in

*a way, the sense of a nation pushing forward, chasing the idea of
what it might be, unable or unwilling to stop itself.*

*Cheers,
TJ*

In June of 2015 I finally passed my real estate exam, and my
income tripled. The first house my mom and I sold that summer was for a couple who were retired and moving to rural
Oregon. This pattern continued all year. Every house we sold
belonged to someone who was moving to the rural Northwest, to Gresham, or to Idaho, or was a house that had been
a rental property that someone wanted to get rid of. None of
these sellers were moving somewhere else in Portland. This
scenario never penciled out for anyone that we worked with.
For months on end, I worked for local buyers, trying to get
them into one-bedroom, nine-hundred-square-foot houses,
houses no bigger than my Hawthorne apartment. They were
always outbid. Some houses had twenty or thirty offers in
on them.

One day my mom and I were sitting in an empty house in
Southwest Portland, listening to the rain falling outside. She
was telling me about her homeless friends. Once a week, she
has lunch with a group of homeless people in a public park
in East County. She likes to say this weekly act of kindness
"feeds her soul."

She told me that Arthur, one of the older homeless men,
had had a stroke and was in the hospital. She told me she was
trying to coordinate a reunion between Arthur and his nine
estranged children.

I tucked my cold feet up underneath me and listened as
best as I could. I always have a mix of sorrow and anger when

I hear the stories my mother tells me about her homeless friends. It makes me sad when I hear about their troubled lives and seemingly intractable problems. It makes me angry when I hear about how the cops routinely arrest and harass them and steal their few belongings. But I've never met any of them, and have a hard time keeping them straight. Except in this case, Arthur—I remembered him; he was the longest homeless resident of the woods near the park. This area near the Sandy *was* his home. He'd lived there for twenty-five years. I was amazed every time I thought about it; he'd managed to support himself camping outside for a quarter-century.

I asked her some more questions and my mom told me about his condition and her plans to help him.

"You know the cops found his camp," my mom said.

"What?"

"Yeah, they stole all his stuff. Arthur camps so far out into the woods, he always thought they'd never find him." My mom raised her eyebrows and shrugged. "They finally found him. And now he's had a stroke and is in the hospital. When they release him, he'll have nowhere to go."

The razing of Arthur's camp seemed symbolic to me. Arthur had been the last crawdad.

When I'm an old lady, maybe I will point out the window in the direction of Arthur's camp. I will point out over the fields near where the Sandy meets the Columbia River, over the gray asphalt and the alder trees and golden grass. "That's where the old man used to live," I will say. "When I was a young woman, my mother used to bring him food. But eventually the cops found his secret camp and he died of a broken heart."

Love
and Filth

I CAN'T SLEEP. It's been two months since you and I broke up. I'm up in the middle of the night looking at my Instagram account. My Instagram account is how I keep track of time.

I also have this app on my phone called Timehop. It shows me what I posted on social media on this particular day of the year for as far back as my accounts go. Mine syncs with Twitter, Instagram, and Facebook. Six years for me.

Tonight, as I look at my phone in the darkness, I see that on this day last year I was making copies of the twenty-third issue of my zine. I also ran into a friend who makes comics at the copy shop and marked "Yes" on an invite to a party that I didn't end up going to.

Two years ago I posted something about italics and sleeping in public.

Three years ago I posted nothing.

Four years ago I posted something about my toenail growing back in.

Pretty mundane stuff.

And then sometimes out of nowhere I will stumble across: "I don't care who blocks me, my heart is breaking!"

And other mortifying emotional diarrhea, if not actual diarrhea.

Sometimes on a given day every post for the last four years will be me complaining about my health. Or me posting about an event that I didn't end up going to. Patterns begin to emerge. To make matters worse, since we broke up near our one-year anniversary, just as I was trying to heal and move on, pictures of us from when we first met each other started popping up. It was awful. I contemplated deleting the app. *No*, I told myself. *You are strong enough for Timehop.*

Anyway, I don't know why I am telling you any of this. It was the kind of thing that bored you when we were together. Of course, when we were together, you would never admit to being bored by anything I said.

I still haven't fallen asleep. I try to think about something else. But my mind goes back to your room. I remember how when I walked into your bedroom for the first time it felt like home. It was a chaotic, jumbled mess of beautiful half-finished paintings, healthy succulents, laundry, and salvaged furniture. It smelled like dirt and candles. It felt like home.

I once told you that I fell in love with you on our third date, on top of Mount Tabor. We had a picnic. You'd made chicken salad for me and it was delicious. I almost cried, tasting it, telling you how much I appreciated the care you put into the meal.

Later you would tell me that you'd obsessed over the food, imagining me chewing it and swallowing it. "This food will be in her body later tonight," you'd said to yourself.

I remember thinking at the time that you were one of the most giving and unselfish people I had ever met. Later, after we broke up, I imagined you sticking your fingers in the food and licking them as you prepared the chicken salad in your small and often dirty kitchen. It grossed me out thinking about it in that way, even though I knew that's how it probably went down.

Of course it also felt familiar, like you felt to me. Like the gallons of milk my family used to leave on the dining room table, unrefrigerated for hours, our ten toothbrushes crammed into one moldy cup on the bathroom counter,

you were the chicken soup my mom would make from picked-over rotisserie birds, meals filled with love and filth, a house brimming with chaos and emotion.

While you were practicing with the band in your garage, I took a shower and waited for you in your bed. When you came inside me, your tooth exploded. Or rather, the place where the tooth had been, before being pulled at the dentist's the week before. The space that had been healing ever since. Something came out, shifted.

I could see your tongue searching for your missing tooth. "Are you okay?" I said.

"I think it might just be scab juice or something," you said, holding your face.

Later that day, when I went to the bathroom, a little bit of you came out of me. It'd been a few hours since I'd seen you but I still smiled. Like I knew a secret about you that you didn't even know about yourself.

You once told me that you had a dream where you were trying to go down on me but I wouldn't stop angrily ranting about some political issue.

"I just wanted to have sex," you said and laughed.

I try to sleep but I miss you. It's only been twelve weeks. It's been over twelve weeks. I know this because the day after we broke up I posted a photo of a tree slowly growing through a chain-link fence. In the picture, the fence is halfway through the tree. I remember thinking that one day it would emerge out the other side. Freedom from the fence in the end, but it seemed like a painful process for the tree. I wondered how the fence felt being stuck inside the tree.

Remember when my mother hired you to draw caricatures at the neighborhood association picnic? When you drew someone my mother knew, a middle-aged woman with thick glasses and no chin, you made her look twenty years younger. She knew it was a false image, but she was grateful. I never told you this, but I remember thinking: *Maybe this is why I love him*; *he reflects back the image of myself that I want to see.* I was afraid of this thought and pushed it aside.

I remember all the wonderful things you told me. And then I remember when you told me I smelled like shit. We were driving down to San Francisco, and out of the blue you told me that I smelled bad and needed to pay more attention in the shower. I still can't figure out if you told me that because you were planning on breaking up with me, if you just wanted to be mean, or if I did actually smell like shit, which was certainly a possibility. I wanted to insult you back, but instead I just apologized. I could tell you were surprised by my reaction and you tried to take it back. But there are no take-backs as far as shit is concerned.

I could have told you how gross it was that you drank straight from the juice container. But I guess I did tell you that. And it was your juice, anyway, why did I care?

But remember? When we first got together and you took me to your friend's wedding? We'd been so in love, dancing until both of us were dripping with sweat. My hair was sloppy and slicked to my forehead and I knew that I probably looked disgusting and drunk but I didn't care because I was so happy. We tried to sleep in the back of your roommate's van in the parking lot, but the attendant spotted us when we got out to pee in the gravel and asked us to leave. We ended up driving out on the country roads for forty minutes looking for a place to pull over and sleep. In the darkness, with the white lines unfurling in front of us, you told me that we should have kids together.

But before that, do you remember what happened right after the wedding? There was that annoying woman standing in front of us by the outdoor fire pit. She wasn't a guest of the wedding, she was just some random person. Remember her? She kept hopping around in front of us and staring at us. She was wearing a white tank top and black leggings. She was very thin and seemed drunk.

"This fire is burning through my pants! But I'm so cold!" she whined. She started shivering and rubbing her shoulders, hopping from one foot to the other. She kept repeating herself. I found her very irritating. I snuggled up closer to you. I felt like telling her that she wasn't wearing pants anyway, those were fucking leggings.

I could tell that she sensed my annoyance and her demeanor changed. "You two are very in love," she said, pointing at us. She stopped her hopping and stood very still and straight.

You and I both smiled and nodded. I felt a little embarrassed to be called out like this by a stranger, but I also knew that if she was going to start the conversation this way, then I had no choice but to engage. And I knew that she knew.

"Yes," I said and looked at you. "We are in love." It was a happy statement, but at the time it felt as if she were pulling something out of me. Like she was a kid trying to bum a cigarette from me.

"I'm an Empath," the woman said. "That's what I do for a living. I can sense things about people and you two are very in love."

Oh brother, I thought.

She squinted at us. "In fact," she went on, "I think you will make a very good couple. In fact, I think that you are so in love that you poop with the bathroom door open!" The Empath smiled. "You love each other so much that you will just love to talk about your shit all the time."

"Well, I don't think we've gotten to that stage yet," I remember muttering, even though I knew she was right.

The Empath laughed and threw her head back. "Yes! All you will do is talk about your shit. You won't be able to stop talking about your shit together … what it feels like, what it smells like. That is how close you will be. That's how much you love each other."

Age Is Just a Number, Gresham Is Just a State of Mind

82ND AVENUE RUNS NORTH AND SOUTH through East Portland, straight as an arrow, no deviation whatsoever until it merges with I-205 in Clackamas.

It's a simple thing: a four-lane highway, a turn lane in the middle, flanked on either side by used car lots, strip malls, and Chinese buffet restaurants. Everyone knows what 82nd Avenue is. And everyone knows what it means. It's where you go to get hookers and drugs. It's where Portlandia ends and Portland begins.

On the other hand, the boundary between Gresham and Portland—that isn't so simple. From its northern border at Marine Drive, it jigs and jags east and west, arbitrarily back and forth from around 162nd Avenue to as far east as 185th all the way down to Foster. Many Portlanders and most newly arrived Portlanders are only vaguely aware of this boundary. Most reference anything east of 82nd as Gresham, not realizing that Gresham doesn't begin for another hundred blocks or so. But it's easier that way. And besides, what does it matter? They never go there. Why would they? There's nothing out there except WinCos and racists.

I used to run a monthly storytelling event at an old diner above the Sandy River called Tad's Chicken 'n Dumplins. I called it Tad's Talks. It was very easy to get to Tad's if you lived in Portland. All you had to do was jump on I-84 for twenty minutes and get off at exit 18 near the Troutdale outlet malls. But it was a constant struggle to promote the event. One of my performers actually admitted to me that she had made a special trip to the grocery store so she could buy "snacks for the drive" in case she got hungry. She didn't realize that Tad's was so close to her house in Portland. And so it seemed that a major part of running the event was teaching people where, in fact, they were.

My ex-boyfriend John had three cats. The two orange tabbies had normal names: Felix and Marcus. But he'd named the chubby gray male with the bent tail Gresham. John thought it was funny. And admittedly Gresham was a funny cat. He had a cute personality and was always covered in crumbs and dandruff since he was too chubby to clean himself properly. During our relationship, it was hard not to feel like Gresham—the city and the cat—was the butt of every joke.

When John and I broke up I had to move in with my parents in Gresham. They live near the City Park—the nice part of Gresham—but Gresham nonetheless. For a while I thought my life was over. Fortunately my parents and I eventually finished a kitchen on my side of their house, blocked off a door, and now I have a sliding scale one-bedroom apartment for less than five hundred dollars a month. For a while I thought I'd move out of my parents' duplex and back into Portland, but checking Craigslist rentals periodically has cured me of this folly. Sure, I could move in with some kids in St. Johns or Montavilla, or with some uptight people my own age who are allergic to everything and require me to be spiritual or vegan … or I could stay put.

I met my most recent boyfriend on OkCupid. Our first date was a month before my thirty-fourth birthday. I went on to spend most of the next year at his apartment in Southeast Portland, and then last May I was single again a month before my thirty-fifth birthday, and living full time again in Gresham.

I have come to appreciate Gresham, its diversity, its lack of pretension, and its cheap housing. And when I think about what I give up by living in Gresham, it still makes sense for me to stay put. To be clear, I do give up a lot: I give up proximity to Portland, where my friends and most of the dateable men live. Nearly all the men in Gresham sport goatees, baseball caps, fish they've reeled in, cars, and ATVs in their online dating profiles. And driving into Portland and meeting someone for an unsuccessful date is far more disappointing when it takes me forty-five minutes just to get there.

The month I turned thirty-five I got my real estate license and became my mother's business partner. Shortly after, she and I listed a house on 83rd in Southeast Portland. It was a nice house, one hundred years old. We listed it for $275,000.

A few weeks later we had to ask the owners for a price reduction. It turns out that people aren't willing to pay very much for a house a block on the wrong side of 82nd, especially if it faces a used car lot.

I thought the house was worth every penny. In fact I took it personally that people would reject a perfectly good house because of circumstances beyond the house's control. But it wasn't my call; if we wanted to sell a house on the wrong side of 82nd, we had to expect less in return. We lowered the price and got an offer almost immediately.

Meanwhile I got back on OkCupid. I felt I was emotionally ready to date again and I was starting to feel good about my career in real estate. But after I set up my profile and chose my pictures, I hardly got any messages and the messages I did get were all from extremely handsome men from foreign countries. I couldn't understand what had changed since the last time I'd used the site a year and one month earlier. My pictures were actually better now than they used to be. I'd finally quit smoking. I'd become a professional. I was working out.

What the hell was going on?

And then it struck me. What had changed was that time had passed. I was now thirty-five. Not thirty-three. Men must draw an arbitrary line at thirty-four. And I was just on the other side by a month or so. And the men from foreign countries? They probably figured I was an old maid by now, desperate, with nothing to lose. I felt dejected; in the year that had passed since the last time I had used the dating site, I had moved from  one side of 82nd to the other side. Heck, I might even be in Gresham. No one could be sure and no one cared to find out.

I realized I had been doing the same thing on the site myself; my criteria specified that I was only looking for men from thirty-three to forty-two years old. But why stop at forty-two? What was so special about that age? Probably nothing. It's just that it's a slippery slope. You start out at 33rd and Clinton and you end up at 122nd and Stark and then where the hell are you? I mean, would I even be able to have sex with someone that old? Have they taken care of their teeth? I mean, let's be real here.

I began to suspect that other things on my profile might be driving away traffic from my listing. For example, one of the most degrading aspects of OkCupid is that you have to choose a body type. You can be fit, athletic, jacked, skinny, average, overweight, a little extra, etc. Hardly anyone describes themselves as overweight. I checked average. Technically I am overweight, but to be overweight in the United States is to be merely average because most people are overweight. And all my female friends say, "Martha, you are *not* overweight." And I say, yes, according to my BMI I am overweight. And then they say, "Yes, but you are not *overweight.*" And then we both repeat ourselves over and over until one of us says, well, they are doing research now that says that those weight charts are bullshit anyway and we laugh and change the subject.

Meanwhile, I get stood up. Meanwhile men just simply don't write back. Or they carry on a pleasant weeklong back and forth only to announce that they are emotionally unavailable and really shouldn't be on OkCupid to begin with. My second date tells me right to my face that he doesn't want to go on another date with me. I have never experienced this before. I have always been the one to reject my dates. Seriously. I don't like how it feels. It fucking sucks.

Meanwhile, my mother and I list a house and it sells in two days.

I've been working with a client who is repeatedly getting outbid by thirty, forty, fifty thousand dollars. Or she views a house and is thinking about putting an offer on it only to discover that it's already pending and is no longer available. A different client puts in an offer and it turns out he can't afford the house because his funding falls through. It's not a buyer's market in Portland. There are too many people looking for housing and not enough houses to go around. The fixer-uppers are going for cash to investors and the ones that can be financed are too expensive for many first-time homebuyers.

I contemplate setting up another OkCupid profile and changing my age just to see if I get different results. I stop trying to seem pleasant to the men on the site, and start openly mocking them if they send me idiotic messages. Sometimes all I do is type "ha ha" and let them figure it out. My friend Camille once told me that her thirties were her worst decade for dating. "Just wait until you hit forty," she told me. "Everyone is getting their first divorce and no one thinks that you are desperately trying to find someone to have kids with. It's much better."

Maybe as a young blond woman I have been in a seller's market for so long that I don't know how to behave now that I suddenly find myself in a buyer's market. I consider quitting OkCupid until I can lose thirty pounds. Taking myself off the market to do a remodel, so to speak. I look into whitening my teeth. I start working out every day and start losing weight. I buy myself some new clothes.

This morning I'm meeting my buyer at a house out on 118th and Bush Street off Powell. As I pull up in my car I laugh out loud because the house for sale is literally right next door to my grandma's old house. I practically grew up in that house. But the neighborhood got bad for a while, and my grandma moved to Gresham about twelve years ago because there was a boarded-up meth house across the street. But maybe the neighborhood has gotten better? I don't know. By law I'm not allowed to comment on crime in any given neighborhood.

This house my client is looking at has been on the market for a month and hasn't gotten a single offer. This is unusual in Portland's hot housing market. The listing agent believes it's because there are only one and a half baths and most people prefer a master bedroom with a bathtub. They've recently reduced the price by ten thousand dollars.

We go inside. The house is big and a little funky. The owner used to raise St. Bernards and there is some heavy-duty fencing going on outside. The kitchen is seriously outdated. But there are hardwood floors and a nice detached garage. The owners are there to show us around and they seem very nice and a little desperate—it's odd that they haven't vacated the house during our appointment. The whole time we're inside, my client and I never have a moment to ourselves to talk about the house.

Back outside in the car my client is nervous. She's been rejected so many times before. And why has the house been on the market so long? Is there something wrong with it? Is there something wrong with the neighborhood? What should she do? The price has already been lowered. The owners are motivated to sell. I wonder why she is being so wishy-washy and then I realize that for the first time in her search she knows that if she puts an offer in, she actually might get this house. Is it what she really wants?

A man who was thirty percent my enemy asked me that same question the other day. "Why are you on here? You are cute and interesting-seeming." It was obviously a message that he had cut and pasted to a thousand women, hoping someone would reply. And I wanted to say: "Why do you think? I'm on here for the same reason you are."

Maybe it's not ever been a seller's market, but my standards have gotten way higher since my twenties. Or maybe I've just been on the market so long people figure there's something wrong with me. Or maybe it's not even about real estate at all. It's actually a rental market that I should be talking about. Maybe I've been looking for investors or motivated buyers when actually I should be looking for reliable, clean, honest renters. Maybe it's about renting temporarily. It doesn't have to be a long-term relationship, just a safe space for now. Maybe it's about making myself look affordable, clean, and convenient. Maybe I should lower my standards about what kind of renters I will accept. Maybe I should just skip the background check and the credit check.

Wait.

Wait just a minute.

I'm not a fucking house. Thank god, I'm not a fucking house.

Acknowledgments

I'd like to thank The Sisterhood, TJ Acena, Michael Heald, Aaron Miller, Jessie Carver, and my family.

Updates

At the back of my first book there were several personals ads. While illustrating new ads for this book, I began to wonder what impact—if any—the old ads have had on my friends' lives over these past five years.

LIZZY: After my ad ran in *One More for the People*, I had a string of terrible relationships. While I can't say for sure this was Martha's fault, it's easier for me to blame her than to take responsibility. Now I'm in an LTR with a midwesterner, which I also blame on Martha.

VINH: My personals ad in *One More for the People* was the redheaded stepchild of my many dating profiles. Five years later and here I am with not one but two actual redheaded stepchildren. My girlfriend denies having read the ad back then, but I think the timing works out.

The following ads are, once again, real people looking for love.

I am a woman on the verge of a nervous breakdown, thirty-six years old, mother to one short-legged dog. I am in search of someone who is over six feet tall (this is negotiable) who enjoys being interesting and is not threatened by a feminist killjoy. Also, must know that existence is plagiarism. About me: Why bother?

annmarieomalley@gmail.com

Mary Higgins—SWQF—33

m a single, independent, proud, sapiosexual woman in my thirties. People
sually describe me as kind, sweet, and intelligent. I'm a cute-as-fuck chub-
y chick with a love of taking care of others. I'm a writer, artist, zinester, and
:acher. In my own time I enjoy reading long books, playing video games,
nd cooking good food. I like simple dates, like dinner and a movie, but
njoy the effort put into more adventurous moments such as hiking, swim-
ing, or ice skating. Originally from Texas, I have a soft spot for my family
nd a love of nature. I'd like a partner more into long talks than long walks
n the beach. I'm a stickler for charged opinions, and look forward to being
ith someone who has just as much to teach me as I'm willing to learn. I'm
proud feminist, and will take nothing less than what I deserve in a part-
er, that is kindness, respect, and equity. Are you up for the challenge?
iggins.mary@gmail.com

Julia is a neurotic cat-lady with chronic pain and delusions of grandeur. She enjoys being spoiled, wined and dined, and treated like a princess. She is looking for an intellectual equal, a creative-minded person who is genuine and enjoys doing the dishes. PROS: Julia is fun, nasty, sweet, and sexy. CONS: Julia is not a morning person and hates to clean. If you can handle the CONS, Julia may be interested in allowing you to entertain her over a five-course meal. If the conversation goes well, you have great style, and can make her laugh—anything is possible. All are welcome to apply.

julialaxer@gmail.com

Thirty-one-year-old editor/writer in Portland, Oregon, seeking a man or woman who preferably lives within lazy biking distance … will drive across town for the right person. Bonus points if you'll play chess and go camping with me. Must like spicy food and excessive amounts of books and plants. It's likely that I won't get your witty pop-culture references but I have other redeeming qualities and I promise to not judge your grammar—no, really! I am very independent and need far more alone time than the average person but I'm excellent at feigning being extroverted. I also take full responsibility for incidental typos in this book, and would like to apologize preemptively to Martha for any you might find.

jessiecarver@gmail.com

Martha Grover is the author of *One More for the People.* She has been publishing her zine *Somnambulist* since 2003. She lives in Gresham, Oregon.

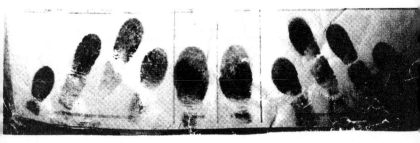

PO BOX 14871 PORTLAND, OREGON 97293